THE BEETLE EXPERIENCE

A Memoir–Play Hybrid

By Dana Morrison

THE BEETLE EXPERIENCE
Living with Laughter. Dying with Peace.
© 2025 by Dana Morrison
All rights reserved. Published 2025.

DO NOT REPRODUCE WITHOUT PERMISSION

The design elements of this book were produced with the help of AI.

Published in the United States of America by

 SPIRITMEDIA

Spirit Media, Inc.
https://spiritmedia.us

Spirit Media and our logos are trademarks of
Spirit Media, Inc.
8045 Arco Corporate Drive STE 130
Raleigh, NC 27617
1-888-800-3744

Biographies & Memoirs | Religious | Christian

Paperback ISBN: 979-8-89307-190-0
eBook ISBN: 979-8-89307-191-7
PDF ISBN: 979-8-89307-192-4
Library of Congress Control Number: 2025917180

DEDICATION

This book is dedicated to Mary Ellen Whiteman to celebrate the life of Stephen Michael Bailey, more commonly known as "Beetle." Without your inspiration, I might never have written the accounts of a man you hold so dear to your heart.

Dear Audience,

Whether you knew Beetle or not, I hope that you will receive the blessing of laughter and be inspired to finish well in the race in which you find yourself.

May you endure to the end, running with diligence, and seek Almighty God on the journey.

Sincerely,

Dana Morrison

EPIGRAPH

A cheerful heart is good medicine. (Proverbs 17:22)

Beetle is living *proof.*

"It wasn't me!"— Beetle

PREFACE
WHY THIS BOOK IS TOLD THIS WAY

Some stories are too full of laughter to be told quietly. Some lives are too bright to be dimmed by paragraphs alone.

This book began as a collection of memories — funny, raw, sacred, and real — about a man named Beetle, and how God used him to shape my life. At first, it seemed like a memoir. But every time I tried to write it that way, it felt too small. Beetle isn't a man who speaks in paragraphs. He speaks in stories. Scenes. Punchlines. Pranks. And sometimes, the kind of silence that says more than words ever could.

So I started writing what I remembered — as I remembered it. Not always perfectly. Not always linearly. But truthfully. And soon, I found myself not just telling stories, but *staging* them. Dialogue came alive. Friends stepped forward again. Laughter echoed. And tears found their way in, too.

That's when I realized: this isn't just a book.

It's a **memoir–play hybrid** — meant to be read, remembered, performed, or passed along.

I invite you to read this like a story that's still unfolding. Because it is.

And if you find yourself laughing, or weeping, or hearing Beetle's voice in your head — then you're exactly where you're meant to be.

Welcome to *The Beetle Experience*.

SO TAKE YOUR SEAT. THE CURTAIN IS RISING.

HOW TO READ THIS BOOK

The Beetle Experience is not a traditional memoir, and it is not a conventional stage play either. It is something in between — a blend of memory and performance, of lived experience and dramatized reflection.

You'll notice that the format shifts between:

- **MEMOIR NARRATION (DANA):** Prose passages where Dana retells events from memory.

- **DRAMATIC SCENES:** Dialogue that brings Stephen (Beetle), Jimmy, and others to life on stage.

- **STAGE DIRECTIONS:** Visual cues that show how this story could be performed as well as read.

- **TABLEAUX, MONOLOGUES, AND VIGNETTES:** Theatrical forms used to freeze a moment, give voice to a single character, or highlight a brief snapshot of Beetle's story.

- **READER'S NOTES:** Prose-only sections that give factual context (time, place, and significance).

Why this style? Because Beetle's story is more than a sequence of events. It is a performance of life itself: full of laughter, mystery, mischief, and the quiet strength of faith.

However you choose to receive it, remember this:

- **You are part of the audience.**

- **You are part of the memory.**

- **You are welcome in *The Beetle Experience*.**

WHO IS BEETLE?

DEFINITION

Beetle — noun, a laughter-generating, treasure-hunting, car-re-building, churchgoing, movie-quoting, sasquatch-hunting, model rocket-making, bundle of laughter... and the best friend of a man named Dana.

Used in a sentence: *"It was the worst day of my life, then Beetle showed up and it was the best."*

NOTE

The only ones I know that didn't refer to him as Beetle were his old-est brother, Jimmy, and his next oldest brother, Mark. They mostly called him Stephen, or Steve. I'm not sure why. My guess is that since Jimmy and Mark did not get much of a chance to witness Ste-phen's life in the Danforth area, they simply knew him as Stephen.

Whatever name you know him by — *STEPHEN, STEVE, OR BEETLE* — *One thing is certain: he made you laugh.*

GLOSSARY OF
THEATRICAL TERMS

MEMOIR NARRATION – DANA speaking directly from memory, retelling events in past tense.

TABLEAU – A staged "living picture," actors freeze to capture a visual moment.

SILENT TABLEAU – A frozen stage picture without dialogue, emphasizing posture and expression.

MONOLOGUE – A speech by one character offering insight, story, or emotion.

VIGNETTE – A short, self-contained snapshot capturing a single moment or impression.

CAMEO – A brief appearance by a non-central character that adds humor or recognition.

Table of Contents

ACT I
The Pre-Beetle Days.

"Oh my head!" – Stephen

CREATED FOR JOY

In the beginning, God created the heavens and the earth.

Then He made Beetle.

Scripture tells us in Proverbs 17:22 that *"A cheerful heart is good medicine."*

In Stephen Bailey, God created a medicine man — and one highly proficient in his work.

> *For we are God's handiwork, created in Christ Jesus to do good works, which God prepared in advance for us to do.* (Ephesians 2:10)

God imparted humor to mankind, and to Stephen He gave a super-heaping dose. From birth to his final breath, Beetle is living joy.

And so began a life of laughter that would ripple through family, friends, and faith alike.

This is where the story starts.

Scene 1: Getting Warmed Up

MEMOIR NARRATION (DANA): *You've taken your seat now in the front row of The Beetle Experience. It is a small theater with a small stage. A velvety red curtain remains closed and light music plays in the background. Neighboring members of the audience chit-chat with small-town talk and you feel right at home. Coming into the theatre is like putting on comfortable slippers.*

STAGE ACTION: The music and the lights fade in unison. The conversations come to a lull. Everyone anticipates what will happen next. You hear the flick of a spotlight which warms to a glow pointing skyward.

STAGE LIGHTS: Heavenly glow.

GOD:

Have you considered what I am doing with this man, Stephen?

SATAN (hissing):

Yesss, I despise his sense of humor.

STAGE ACTION: GOD smiles.

STAGE LIGHTS: Spotlight returns to earth and the lights dim again.

STAGE ACTION: Though dark, you can faintly see the curtains opening and you hear the squeak of the curtain's cable being pulled by hand. You again hear the flick of a loud switch operating the spotlight. The yellow glow of the spotlight warms up to a soft circle on the stage with an empty stool. But there is no one there.

STAGE LIGHTS: Spotlight searches left and right.

SOUND EFFECT: SMACK! SLAP! OWE!

STAGE ACTION: There is a chuckle from the audience as if someone tried to give someone a kiss in the dark room and got slapped.

MEMOIR NARRATION (DANA): Oh, that had to be Beetle. Somehow, he was sitting near you in the audience, but he's supposed to be on the stage as Stephen (the name given by his parents).

STAGE ACTION: DANA, from stage, gives a loud whisper.

DANA:

Beetle! I mean, Stephen, get up here!

STAGE ACTION: Audience laughs loudly. STEPHEN sheepishly walks to the stage as his old-character, Stephen, Rubik's cube in hand.

STEPHEN (sheepish):

Who… me?

MEMOIR NARRATION (DANA): You see that he is a young man. Plump. Fair-skinned and freckled. His brown hair is flat on his head. He is wearing an unbuttoned flannel shirt over a dirty work shirt, worn-out blue jeans, and dirty steel-toe boots. He has a folding lock-blade knife in its leather sheath on his belt. The mustache on his thirteen-year-ish face is somewhat thin, but definitely intentional. It has been trying to break free since he was five, only being held back by puberty. As he stands, he occasionally looks to his hands where he is making the last couple moves to solve a Rubik's cube.

STAGE LIGHTS: Spotlight widens.

STAGE ACTION: DANA and STEPHEN are now both on stage, sitting on stools.

DANA (to audience):

Welcome to The Beetle Experience. I am Dana, and this is the star of the show, Beetle… I mean Stephen. I will need to play a couple roles while we watch Stephen's life unfold. One, I will play Stephen's best friend. Two, I will often turn to you, the audience, and narrate as we watch various scenes unfold and give you some backstory here and there. Sit back, relax, and enjoy how God used this best friend in my life as a reflection of His own sense of humor.

STEPHEN (protesting):

What?! So, this is how we are going to do this? I'm the main character?! You never said *I* was going to be the main character!

DANA:

Yup, let's just play it out and live out our fun times together.

STEPHEN:

But me? Why me? You dragged me here for this?! To be made a SPECTACLE of?!

DANA:

No one is making a spectacle of you. We cherish you and the memories of you. Besides, YOU don't have a choice. YOU are what I have left of the memories in my mind and that's it! Got it?! Besides, we are going to go to Taste of China in Houlton as soon as we finish.

STEPHEN (relenting): Well, I guess if we have to. I do like Chinese food and I can snatch up a copy of the Coffee News.

MEMOIR NARRATION (DANA): What you noticed about Stephen was a warm, kind, gentle face and contagious smile. You also saw a unique humility. His smile spoke directly to your heart, saying, "I'll do anything for you." But it wasn't a line he even needed to read. You just knew it.

DANA (to audience):

Welcome to The Beetle Experience. I am Dana, and this is the star of the show, Stephen. We'll call him Stephen, for now at least.

STEPHEN (jumping in):

My dad is the only man I've ever known who got a sunburn on the roof of his mouth.

MEMOIR COMMENTARY (DANA): *The story was true. His dad had been sleeping at the beach and laying in such a way that the sun shone straight up into the top of his mouth while he was snoring away. He got blisters from what I'm told.*

STEPHEN:

My dad was the only guy I know that could look like he was fast asleep in church but could remember every word.

MEMOIR COMMENTARY (DANA): *Also true. My dad, Gerald Morrison, had been a Sunday School teacher for one of the adult classes and recalled that Jimmy could remember in great detail what was being discussed even when he looked like he was fast asleep. Stephen also had this knack and also shared his father's gift of an exceptional memory.*

DANA:

And your dad was a storyteller…

STEPHEN:

Yeah, Dad came home one day laughing up a storm. You tell this one, Dad.

STAGE LIGHTS: A new spotlight. JIMMY SENIOR steps on stage. He is dark haired, wearing a blue button-up shirt and dark pants. He is also plump and soft-spoken. His flat dark hair comes almost to the eyes of his round face. As Jimmy smiles, you can't help but smile in return and you see where Stephen gets many of his physical features.

JIMMY (storytelling):

There was a guy at work that just kept telling these long tales. No one believed him. Story after story, he'd just keep spinnin' unbelievable tales. Well, one day I said to him, "Well, I've got one for ya. Up here we have this creature. It's brown in the summer and white in the winter. Besides having long hairy pointy ears, and big front teeth, in the winter it grows these great big hairy snowshoes on its feet and runs around on the top of the snow."

STEPHEN:

Tell them what he said!

JIMMY:

The guy was baffled and paused, then he said, "I've heard a lot of stories in my day, but I ain't never heard of no creature with hairy long pointy ears and big teeth that grows any big ol' hairy snowshoes on its feet. Ya' got me beat."

SOUND EFFECT: Laughter from the stage and audience.

STEPHEN:

My dad loves music. Though he loved a lot of gospel music, Billy Speer was his favorite.

MEMOIR NARRATION (DANA): *Billy Speer had sung smoothly in a relaxing low tone. He had been a large man with a heart for the Lord even bigger. Billy and his wife, Paula, traveled and sang at churches, conferences, and even at Living Waters, which we will hear about later.*

STEPHEN:

Yeah, if the car was moving, Billy Speer was playing on the 8-track.

MEMOIR FOOTNOTE (DANA): *If you don't know, an 8-track was what existed before we used cassette tapes. If you don't know what cassette tapes* *are, they were used before we had CDs. If you don't know what CDs are, they were used before MP3s. Ask your kids if you aren't sure what MP3s are.*

STEPHEN (closing tribute to dad):

Think of it this way, my dad loved Billy Speer so much, that wherever we went as a family in our car, Billy Speer was there singing to us. It was as if he was in the back seat the whole time.

STAGE ACTION: Spotlight on JIMMY fades as he quietly exits.

DANA (to audience):

You see how that went? Just like that, Jimmy was in the story, then we are back to Beetle, uh I mean, Stephen. That's how it's gonna go. There will be some narration and commentary, there will be live action with Stephen, also known as Beetle, and others on the stage. With that, here we go. Let's all shift to the days before Beetle was known as Beetle.

End of Scene 1

Scene 2: Let the Pranks Begin

MEMOIR NARRATION (DANA): I'm Dana, your narrator, here. The stories you will see are true. The names haven't been changed to protect the innocent as there were likely none that were innocent. In 1987, Stephen had become of legal age to acquire his driver's license, which also became a license to prank. We will pick up the story there, as that was the time our shenanigans really accelerated. Hit the gas, Stephen!

STAGE ACTION: STEPHEN smiles and stomps his boot on the floor, hands at steering-wheel positions ten and two.

STAGE ACTION: SPLIT LEFT – Dana's bedroom with electronics strewn around, wires forming a rudimentary radio antenna on the ceiling, a Commodore 64 home computer on the desk. SPLIT RIGHT – Stephen's living room, TV making background noise, STEPHEN with a phone in hand preparing to dial.

STEPHEN (to audience):

It's cordless. That's a line from Tommy Boy. You gotta see that.

DANA:

Yes, I know you are a movie quoting machine, but let's get to pranking!

STAGE ACTION: STEPHEN dials.

SOUND EFFECT: RING, RING.

DANA (answering):

Hello.

STEPHEN:

May I speak to Dana?

DANA:

Uh, it is me. There's only two of us on stage and you know you aren't really holding a phone, right?

SOUND EFFECT: Chuckles from the audience.

STEPHEN:

Well, I gotta make sure it's you and that I didn't accidentally dial a member of the audience… I have an idea. What ya' doing this Saturday?

DANA:

Not much. What are you thinking?

STEPHEN:

So, Dave, Carl, and Carol are going to some youth conference—I overheard them talking about it. When they are in their little conference, let's go and move one of their vehicles.

DANA:

Absolutely!

MEMOIR COMMENTARY (DANA): *By the way, I was pretty sure that "youth conference" had been code to youth leaders meaning, "a place to get a reprieve from Stephen and Dana. A place to hide. A place to rest." It must also have been a place to confirm whether or not other youths were nearly as bad as we were. I could just imagine Dave, in his highly organized manner, with a clipboard, taking a poll of youth leaders all over the state of Maine, asking, "On a scale of 1 to 10, how well do the kids in your youth group behave?" and "Can you tell me the number of pranks your youth have played on you this year?" While Dave is taking his imaginary poll, Stephen and I are not only plotting—but getting ready to make a strike.*

MEMOIR NARRATION (DANA): *Stephen and I drove out to the church where the conference was held in his early '80s Chevy, a blue Impala that could* *have passed for a police cruiser if it only had the lights. The interior cloth ceiling is floating in the wind, like every other '80s Impala out there. As we go, we listen to Petra (we love Christian Rock). We pulled up quietly to the church where the conference was being held—well, as quietly as possible for an eight-cylinder Impala missing a muffler. We park with the rest of the vehicles, as if we were attendees. We sat and scoped out the situation. When all seemed clear, Stephen and I slipped out of the car and scanned the parking area, which expanded onto the grass around the driveway of the church hosting a quiet place of refuge for good-meaning, well-intended targets of adolescent mischievousness.*

STEPHEN (whispering):

Psst. That is Carol's car.

STAGE ACTION: STEPHEN and DANA try the door. It's locked.

DANA:

I dunno, Stephen… Are we gonna get caught doing this?

STEPHEN:

Aww, c'mon, what's the harm?

DANA (pointing):

There's Carl's car.

STEPHEN:

Saweet!

MEMOIR COMMENTARY (DANA): *His version of "sweet" had an "a" in it. The proper pronunciation is "Suh-wheat," said while emphasizing the "wh" of wheat.*

MEMOIR NARRATION (DANA): *Sure enough, Carl's car had been unlocked. Perfect. Target acquired and locked in. Stephen opened the door, slipped the car into neutral (these were the days before shift and steering-lock mechanisms). Standing at the driver's door, he pushed it backward while I did the* *same at the passenger door. Once it was rolling down the hill, we hopped in. Stephen pumped the brakes, head careened backward, and maneuvered the car into a different spot—perfectly parallel to the others but on the opposite side of the driveway. It would be obvious to Carl this is NOT where he parked his car.*

STEPHEN:

That'll do it!

DANA:

Yeah, Carl's gonna come outta that conference a little confused.

Silence Is Golden

MEMOIR NARRATION (DANA): *One thing was sure: Stephen and I never spoke about our escapades to others unless absolutely necessary. This theatrical version of Stephen's life was a good excuse to tell all.*

STEPHEN:

So now we wait.

MEMOIR NARRATION (DANA): *We had pulled the prank but needed to wait and see what the results would yield. It was like dropping a bomb and waiting for the body count. Not much happens at first. Eventually, tidbits of the story reach us. We pocket each little bit and share them for a chuckle.*

STAGE ACTION: DAVE, CAROL, and CARL appear on stage.

DAVE (looking at Carl):

Carl, are you and Carol available in a few weeks to go to another youth leaders conference?

CARL:

Yeah, I can go!

MEMOIR NARRATION (DANA): *Then we hear it—Carol says:*

CAROL:

Yeah, I can too. But Carl, remember where you park this time!

MEMOIR NARRATION (DANA): *That brings to us a good chuckle, but it was only a taste of what was to come.*

Silence Is a Two-Way Street

MEMOIR NARRATION (DANA): *When pranking, it is important not to slip up and leak intel you do not intend to leak. One must maintain control of their tongue instead of yapping about their youthful exploits. Pulling good pranks also means misinformation campaigns. It was like the secret campaigns of WWII where the United States would stage what looked like military bases with planes, tanks, and hangars—but they were props made of painted wood. Stephen and I were information gatherers. Every time we heard about various youth leader plans and activities, we secretly logged them into our minds. Stephen was the best at this with his exceptional memory. That meant that the youth leaders needed to keep tight lips about any time they were going to a retreat or other event. Hearing that they were going somewhere was most definitely an invitation to prank them.*

End of Scene 2

Scene 3: OIH – Operation Indian House – Pranking Continued

MEMOIR NARRATION (DANA): *While the youth leaders had their "youth conference" code they spoke when crafting plans to escape us, Stephen and I needed our own code. We couldn't afford to slip up and let the enemy know our plans. Now, I know what you must be thinking. Either you are thinking, "Man, you guys were rotten!" or you are thinking, "Wow, my heroes!" Without saying any more, I bet you figured out what our code really meant.*

MEMOIR NARRATION (DANA): *I'm at Stephen's house, hanging out in his messy room that he shared with his next-oldest brother, Mark.*

LYNN (offstage):

STEPHEN MICHAEL BAILEY! You clean that room before you go hanging out with Dana!

MEMOIR NARRATION (DANA): *As we all know, when our parents use our middle names, they mean business. Meanwhile, Stephen's dad would pull me aside and say something like:*

JIMMY SENIOR:

Dana, I'm so glad you're here. You are welcome anytime, and I hope some of your good will rub off on Stephen.

STEPHEN (interrupting):

Yeah, funny you say that because I also remember my dad saying, "I don't know what's worse, either of you guys apart or putting the two of you together."

DANA:

Stephen, yeah, you are right, it must have been before your father got to know me better.

MEMOIR NARRATION (DANA): *Stephen and Mark had beds opposing each other in parallel with a window between them at the head of their beds. Stephen's was on the right, Mark's was on the left.*

STEPHEN:

We need some kind of code for pranking when other people are around.

DANA:

What do you mean?

MEMOIR NARRATION (DANA): *We often had serious conversations in that very configuration.*

STEPHEN:

You know, like when people are going to be going out of town or their cars will be parked somewhere so we can toilet paper them... or maybe TP their houses.

DANA:

Ah, I getcha.

STEPHEN:

Operation Indian House. OIH. I bet no one will figure that out.

MEMOIR NARRATION (DANA): *As the audience, you may have to think about that. Why would we call it Operation Indian House? So, OIH began. While Stephen and I continue to plot on the bed in this scene, I will explain to you: pranks escalate. Maybe you didn't know that. Only the most innocent among you would have been unaware of the natural "bigger and better" of prank-hood. But they did—they got bigger and better while at the same time becoming worse with greater casualties. As mentioned previously, pranking is like nuclear warfare. Once you hit critical mass, it's outta control. Like, World War III outta control.*

STAGE LIGHTS: Spotlight widens: our youth group on stage—kids sitting in metal folding chairs.

STAGE ACTION: DAVE, CAROL, JOY, and CARL are leading in some activities.

MEMOIR NARRATION (DANA): We pulled pranks on youth leaders; they pulled pranks on us. I thought our pranks were worse though. It was as if they had some sort of "Youth Leader Etiquette" constantly tying their hands while at the same time letting us win. But deep down inside, we knew they hated letting us win. Perhaps they thought it had been their service to God to allow us victory.

STEPHEN:

Yeah, like Jesus' statement about turning the other cheek.

MEMOIR NARRATION (DANA): Any time it was mentioned by youth leaders—Dave, Carl, Joy, Carol, or any other prey—that they would be out of town, Stephen would give me a sharp jab with his elbow into my side and say, through the side of his mouth...

STEPHEN (snickering):

OIH.

DAVE:

What are you guys talking about?

MEMOIR NARRATION (DANA): Everyone in the youth group turned to Stephen and me.

STEPHEN:

Oh, nothing.

MEMOIR NARRATION (DANA): Operation Indian House began with a bang. We began mentally locking in, like heat-seeking missiles, the times and places where youth leaders would be and set the targets—cars and houses—dead center in our sights. No real casualties were expected, just the humiliation of coming home to a nice White Cloud. Well, White Cloud wasn't really our choice— Scott toilet paper was the best. You can do a lot with 1,000 sheets per roll. It was an economic and logical choice for the mischievous youthful mind. Toilet papering a home or car, or "rolling" as it is also called (though we didn't personally call it "rolling"), is a true art with techniques that must not be forgotten and should be passed on through generations with proper TP education.

STEPHEN:

What a GREAT idea! Let's start a TP Education Program!

MEMOIR NARRATION (DANA): *Stephen, joining me in narrating now, says—while coming up with the rules off the top of his head:*

STEPHEN (looking up as if reading from a mental list):

When TP-ing a vehicle, or OIH as we call it, remember this:

1. Pretty doesn't matter.

2. Roll over the top of the vehicle, then have someone on the other side of the vehicle to roll it back under. Repeat.

3. Wrap the wiper blades.

4. Wrap the mirrors.

5. Wrap the wheels.

6. Wrap the antenna.

7. The less paint showing, the better.

DANA:

But what about a house?

STEPHEN:

Well, a house is a little different:

1. Practice throwing over the roof until you get it right. It's an art. You want to throw it so the TP is unwinding itself as it flies instead of just breaking.

STAGE ACTION: At this, BEETLE'S and DANA's heads pretend to follow an imaginary arc of streaming white toilet paper across the audience, similar to following a shooting star and lock their glare on the right side of the theater.

SOUND EFFECT: The audience chuckles.

STEPHEN (continues):

2. Have someone on the other side of the home to return throws back to you.

STAGE ACTION: In reverse motion, BEETLE'S and DANA'S heads move back to the left side of the theater following the same arc backwards. The audience chuckles again.

STEPHEN:

3. Trees are considered part of the house, as are shrubs, lawn ornaments, bicycles, etc.

4. Mailboxes count as lawn ornaments.

5. Like with cars, the less you can make out the color of the house, the better.

MEMOIR NARRATION (DANA): Back to the story. Unrelenting flashes of white exploded by way of toilet paper, like the closing scene of War Games when the nuclear bombs are flashing across the map in the War Room. Carl then Dave then Carol then Dave then Dave again then Carol then Carl. House then car then house then house then car and truck and so forth. Target acquired. OIH performed. Mission accomplished. Repeat. Targets would change and sometimes Scott (no pun intended), another good friend, would join us in the action. Retaliatory strikes were limited by way of the law against us minors, so we had a constant upper hand. By the way, pranking is like influenza—it is highly contagious.

After a while, the youth leaders couldn't tell where the pranks were coming from because other youth started getting involved.

STEPHEN:

It was AWESOME!

MEMOIR NARRATION (DANA): *While the audience is laughing about the events playing out on stage, you wonder to yourself, "Is this book just about pranks?"*

STEPHEN:

Yes!

DANA:

Stephen, you know that's not true. This is just part of your story.

STEPHEN: Yeah, you're right, but I do love this part of what you've written!

DANA:

Why thank you! We are going to get into some serious stuff—that will be coming—but we need to finish laying out the backstory. Which means… more pranks!

End of Scene 3

Scene 4: Warning. Don't Try This at Home. It Will Likely Get You Arrested

DANA (to audience):

I must preface the following section with extreme caution and remind our audience that we lived in a much different time in the '80s and '90s than we do today. Treat the following as a historical account. In no way do I condone this sort of activity today.

STAGE ACTION: STEPHEN arrives at my house. STEPHEN and DANA are in Dana's room.

STEPHEN:

Hey, I brought some stuff.

STAGE ACTION: STEPHEN takes things out of a dark-purple knapsack one at a time, making hand motions along the way as if each is some special thing.

STEPHEN:

Here's some wire.

STAGE ACTION: STEPHEN acts like a magician taking things out of his magic hat.

STEPHEN (continuing):

Here's an alarm clock... Here's a model rocket ignitor... Here's some firecrackers... and here's... oh never mind, that's lint.

STAGE ACTION: STEPHEN drops the lint back into his bag.

DANA:

I have here a switch for the door, electrical tape, a big blue capacitor... and another big blue capacitor... and that's it.

STAGE ACTION: STEPHEN and DANA nod in agreement in unison.

STEPHEN & DANA:

Will this even work?

STEPHEN:

Let's do this. Let's try to charge it on a car battery and see.

MEMOIR NARRATION (DANA): We add some long wires to the push-button switch which is wired onto the model rocket ignitor, taped onto the firecracker fuse, wired to the big blue capacitors—and viola! A firecracker-bomb is born. We take it outside to Stephen's car and use a couple wires to charge the capacitor for a moment. I'm holding the push button switch—as when it is re-leased, the circuit will be completed. After a few seconds of charging the capacitor, I let go.

SOUND EFFECT: HISS!

MEMOIR NARRATION (DANA): The HISS from the fuse fills the air along with the puff of light blue smoke from the firecracker and—

SOUND EFFECT: BANG!

MEMOIR NARRATION (DANA): It works.

DANA (to audience):

We immediately went back to my room to put the finishing touch-es, like adding the alarm clock—which was only for looks—on our innocent, but ominous-looking device that in today's world would have landed us in jail. Again, I remind you that this is only intended to produce a harmless CRACK of a firecracker. I can just imagine if anyone pulled this gag today, there would be a SWAT team and a bomb squad showing up and rest assured... SOMEONE would be arrested.

MEMOIR NARRATION (DANA): *The final product? Two big blue cylinders, an alarm clock, and curls of red and black wire that looked like something from an episode of "MacGyver." Then, we just needed to put it in its location and set it up. The church van. Ok, hear that again... THE CHURCH VAN? Wow, we were mischievous and unruly teens. Did I mention that I was a PK (preacher's kid)? We went to the church, located across the street, on a Saturday evening. Dave often drove the van on Sunday mornings to pick up some kids for church, so we thought it would be great to charge it up, set the contraption on the driver's seat, and wire the switch to the driver's door. And do all this from the passenger side of the van so as to not set it off by accident. So that's what we did...*

MEMOIR NARRATION (DANA): *Sunday morning rolled around, and we waited on pins and needles.*

STEPHEN:

I'm on pins.

DANA:

I'm on needles.

MEMOIR NARRATION (DANA): *Finally, news arrived.*

STAGE ACTION: DAVE pulls STEPHEN and DANA aside in the church foyer.

DAVE:

Do you guys have any idea who made this?

STEPHEN (dead serious):

Uh, no, what is it?

MEMOIR NARRATION (DANA): *At that point, I lose it. I couldn't contain the laughter. Very often for me, Stephen's wit and candor could set me off. For a while I can hold the serious look, but then I see Stephen's expression and the* *way he said something so convincingly—and the wondering of how he has this superpower—set me into laughter myself. Dave knew with utmost certainty that Stephen and I were the culprits. Of course, we equally knew that he knew we were the culprits. My laughter had to have been a dead giveaway. Oh, the tears. However, we also learned that it didn't work.*

STAGE ACTION: DAVE plops five pounds of failure back into STEPHEN'S hands.

DAVE:

Well boys, I don't know what it was supposed to do, but whatever it was, it didn't work.

STAGE ACTION: DAVE departs.

STEPHEN (to Dana):

Back to the drawing board, I guess.

MEMOIR NARRATION (DANA): *Back at my house, we tested it again. It worked fine. We set it up again the following weekend.*

DANA:

But there was a problem…

STEPHEN:

Yeah, Dave wasn't driving the van that particular Sunday. It was Joy.

DANA & STEPHEN:

Whoops.

STAGE ACTION: THE FOLLOWING SUNDAY.

DAVE:

Um… Joy found this in the van. Good thing it didn't work.

MEMOIR NARRATION (DANA): *Initially, we were concerned that a woman had found it. So, we stopped dead in our tracks and didn't try it anymore.*

STEPHEN:

What!? Yeah, right! That ain't gonna stop us!

STAGE ACTION: STEPHEN and DANA look at each other and nod in unison.

MEMOIR NARRATION (DANA): *Again, we test. It works fine. Again, we set it up.*

STAGE ACTION: AGAIN, THE FOLLOWING SUNDAY.

DAVE:

Nope. I think you guys need to find a new hobby.

MEMOIR NARRATION (DANA): *In further investigation, we discovered something critical: the capacitor only holds a charge for an hour at most before dissipating. Now, if you have a mischievous mind like us, you will probably recognize a critical flaw in our logic. If we really wanted success, all we needed to do was use the cigarette lighter in the van to kick off the model rocket lighter to kick off the firecracker, then just put the bomb-looking device on the driver's seat. But, if we did any damage to the cigarette lighter socket, the deacons would have been sure to discover it and then we would have really been in trouble (just joking, deacons!). With that, we had continued searching for a new way to get Dave.*

End of Scene 4

Scene 5: Dave Buys a New Truck

MEMOIR NARRATION (DANA): *Dave bought a new-to-him truck. A grey Chevy. Dave was very proud of his purchase and had scrimped to purchase it.*

STEPHEN:

OIH.

DANA:

Who?

STEPHEN:

Dave. Not a traditional OIH, but a different prank.

DANA:

Okay, what are you thinking?

STEPHEN:

I'll come get you on Saturday.

MEMOIR NARRATION (DANA): *Stephen had hatched a plan and knew some details that I didn't. Dave was going to park his new-to-him truck at the Ed (or Education) Building and pick it up around 9:00 p.m. after some event. The Ed Building was a building used for Sunday school and Youth Group next to WWBC (Woolwich Wiscasset Baptist Church, the church we attended). Stephen came by my house to pick me up at about 7:00 p.m. that Saturday.*

DANA:

I'm going out Mom, I'll be back in a couple hours.

MEMOIR NARRATION (DANA): *Stephen drove me over to the church and we parked in the old church garage area. It was a mostly abandoned area that had been previously used for working on church buses. Stephen often parked* there to keep his car unnoticed whenever we did pranks near the church. As we left Stephen's car, he reached into the back seat and grabbed a soda can. As we walked down to the Ed Building, where we had already observed our target's truck backed into a parking spot, Stephen started grabbing little bits of rock and gravel from the driveway and put them into the can. It didn't matter that the truck was locked. Stephen didn't need access to the inside, just the outside.

DANA:

What are you going to do?

STEPHEN:

You'll see.

MEMOIR NARRATION (DANA): *Stephen lays down on the ground next to the driver's rear tire of Dave's new truck and ties a soda can, that rattles with rocks and sand, just on the inside of the wheel. Then he goes around the truck looking at the rear tire from various angles and finally says with confidence:*

STEPHEN:

He'll never see it.

DANA:

What now?

STEPHEN:

We watch!

MEMOIR NARRATION (DANA): *A prank like this needed to be witnessed. Fortunately for us, the Ed Building was usually left unlocked. Click. That night was no different. It was about 7:30 p.m. and Dave wouldn't be back for another 90 minutes to discover a noise-making problem with his new truck. Not a problem for us. With Stephen, laughter is like air… it fills the space allotted. We hung out and waited, telling stories, and making wisecracks. It started to get dark and the light in the parking lot kicked on. Then just like that, time had* *passed and there was Dave, being dropped off by Carl in the parking lot. Dave started to go to his truck but turned towards the Ed Building.*

STEPHEN (commanding):

Oh no! Quick, follow me.

MEMOIR NARRATION (DANA): Dave was coming into the Ed Building, probably to use the bathroom before going home.

STEPHEN (whispering):

Let's go to the ladies' room. He won't go in there, he'll go to the men's if he has to use the bathroom.

MEMOIR NARRATION (DANA): So that's what we did. Without making a sound, Stephen and I waited in the ladies' room while Dave used the men's room. We heard a flush, a clearing of a throat, then the creak of the bathroom door. Finally, we heard him leave the building. Now, consider for a moment what might have happened if Dave went into the ladies' room.

STEPHEN (narrating):

One, that would make Dave kinda weird. Two, it would have made Dana and I look pretty weird. Three, worst of all! The prank would have been stopped in its tracks!

STEPHEN:

Phew! That was close. Quick! We don't want to miss it!

MEMOIR NARRATION (DANA): We hurried quietly out to the window that we were using just minutes previously that faced the parking lot. We got there just in time to watch Dave walk around his truck. As with all our youth leaders, the poor guy was probably paranoid. They call it PTPD, "Post-Traumatic Prank Disorder." Satisfied that it was untouched, Dave hopped in the driver's seat, started the truck, and then took off.

SOUND EFFECT: TRUCK RATTLING.

STAGE ACTION: As quickly as DAVE took off, we saw the brake lights and the truck come to a full stop. He didn't get twenty feet when he hit the brakes and put the truck in park.

SOUND EFFECT: RATTLING STOPS.

MEMOIR NARRATION (DANA): *Dave got out and walked around the truck. He looked under the truck. Then he got in the truck and began to go again. This time he went a little more slowly. Stephen and I began to laugh.*

SOUND EFFECT: RATTLING BEGINS AGAIN.

MEMOIR NARRATION (DANA): *He got maybe another twenty feet and we saw brake lights. He got out again. He looked around the truck again. He got back in again. Stephen and I laughed again, but that time a little louder. Then he drove to the main road but was still visible. He stopped yet again. He got out again. He looked around the truck again. Then he got in again and sped off. Stephen and I laughed again, a hysterical violent laughter that just could not be contained. It was the kind of laughter that all you need is the slightest trigger to begin all over again, like a hair trigger.*

DANA:

What do you think Dave is thinking right now?

STEPHEN:

I bet he's going home and looking up the number for the dealer he bought the truck from.

STEPHEN AND DANA (together):

Ahhh… That was good!

MEMOIR NARRATION (DANA): *About now, you might be convinced, as you have watched all this play out before your very own eyes, that Stephen and I loathed our youth leader, Dave, and must have equally loathed Carol and Carl and other youth leaders. That just isn't true. I must say, before diving into an EPIC prank from Dave, that Stephen and I both have a genuine love for Dave,* *our youth leader. Yeah, we tease, chide, prank, and probably have taken many years off his life, but Dave is a true friend. Dave is considerate in whatever our situation. He shows up at random to help in some task. He calls each of us in the youth group to see how we were doing, and he does it with great compassion, while still keeping his humor. He is an excellent example of a man with the calling of Christ in his life. For example, once I was sick with Chicken Pox, Dave brought me a meal. He called it, "Chicken Pox Pie," and as I recall, it was pretty tasty. Likewise, many of us would do just about anything for Dave. If he needed volunteers, Stephen and I would often raise our hands. Then he would say:*

DAVE:

Please, is there anyone else who will volunteer?

MEMOIR NARRATION (DANA): *But he would say that with a good-ol'-Dave smile. Let's not get too mushy about it. Let's leave it at that: we love Dave, he loves us. In further show of his attention to each of us, Dave took the senior guys out on a fishing trip when they graduated. It was a one-on-one male bonding experience of catching trout and tenting in remote Maine. What I remember is having a solid purple ring of blackfly bites around my ankles and cooking up a sucker fish, which I falsely identified as a trout. Besides bringing its own set of stories that each of us senior guys would walk away with, it also deepened our spirituality, friendship, and love for Dave.*

End of Scene 5

Scene 6: Dave Learns Stephen's Kryptonite

MEMOIR NARRATION (DANA): *The war of pranks continued, but honestly, I can't hardly remember the pranks played on us, except a couple. I remember Dave made a fantastic-looking cake for me. He said it was "sponge cake." Sure enough, it was literally made of sponges and impossible to cut despite its delicious-looking frosting. Dave just watched, snickering, while I cut and cut and the cake wouldn't yield to my knife. But one prank Dave pulled tops them all. Let's bring Stephen's mother, Lynn, to the stage.*

STAGE ACTION: Lynn greets the audience with a warm smile.

LYNN (to audience):

Hi! I'm Stephen's mom.

STAGE ACTION: LYNN then turns to DAVE, also on stage.

LYNN:

Hey Dave, I know Stephen and Dana have had a lot of fun pulling all sorts of gags on you. I don't know exactly what they've done, but if you want to get Stephen… I've got a secret.

DAVE (excited):

Oh! I'm all ears!

LYNN:

Stephen loves to sleep in. Some Sunday mornings we can't seem to wake him, nearly making us late for church. Maybe that will give you some ideas.

DAVE:

Thank you, Lynn! That is great information!

MEMOIR NARRATION (DANA): *Stephen loved to sleep in, and when he slept, he slept very soundly. Stephen could saw logs like nobody's business. Legend has it that Stephen could cut down, saw up, split, and stack a cord of wood in a single snore. I kid you not. Armed with some great intel from Stephen's mother, Lynn, Dave hatched a plan. It was the ultimate nuclear weapon in his arsenal that toppled the best prank regimes of the world. Quietly and early one Sunday, Dave showed up at the Bailey house. Lynn eagerly let Dave in, wondering how all this was going to play out. Lynn handed Dave the trombone, ready to go.*

LYNN:

Here's his trombone you asked about. All you gotta do is pucker your lips and blow.

DAVE:

I owe you big, Lynn.

MEMOIR NARRATION (DANA): *Dave crept up the creaky stairs as quietly as possible. He turned to the left, then the left again, and quietly entered Stephen's room with the stealth of an assassin, holding the trombone as the ultimate weapon. You see Stephen's room on stage. Mark's bed on the left. Stephen's on the right. Dave is hunched over, weapon in hand. Dave stands over Stephen, who is fast asleep in the world of axes and chainsaws. Trombone at the ready, Dave is holding in laughter with every fiber of his being.*

DAVE (thinking):

This is it, I can't blow it now.

MEMOIR NARRATION (DANA): *But ironically, he must blow it. Blow the trombone, that is. Stephen, in his dreams, chopped down the entire forest of Allagash, Maine, and provided plenty of firewood to every dreaming human in New England, when shock came across his ears in the form of—*

SOUND EFFECT: BLLLAAA AAHHH!!!

MEMOIR NARRATION (DANA): *In a single moment, Stephen was pulled into reality—the place where dreams are locked up and the tangible* *world collides in a moment of time and causes a detectable rift in the space-time continuum. I'm pretty sure that event was recorded by sensitive NASA equipment. What happened is a once-in-a-lifetime collection of bodily functions, on Stephen's part, permanently logged into ether of space and time. We must slow down the following events on the stage to fully analyze each element that occurs in unison: See how the nervous system in Stephen's body kicks into high gear in a flash, electrifying every synapse of his body with fight, flight, or freeze. Watch how his eyelids snap open in hopes to gather some critical information about the threat his amygdala has made apparent. Keep watching his eyes—instead of gathering information, they bug out of his head temporarily disconnecting his optic nerve, held only by springs, just like the cartoons. BOING! Look how every limb of Stephen's stiffens out straight, like a stick man. Look even closer now, the hair on Stephen's body stands at attention, every follicle. You see one amazing thing that stands out more than any other—Stephen levitates that day. He levitates six or more inches off his bed with a levitation he would not experience again until the Lord took him home in 2023. Then SNAP, just as quickly as that happens, it is over. Stephen's body, now bound by reality, normalizes, and the gift of levitation returns back to the Creator.*

STEPHEN:

OH MY HEAD! Oh my head! My HEAD!

MEMOIR NARRATION (DANA): *Dave had a victorious smile that day, a grin that cannot be washed off. He went to church gleefully telling every listening ear about the event, and everyone was captivated by every detail. I must admit, even I was captivated. Yes, Dave was victorious that day. I'm told that the news of Dave's victory over Stephen traveled like wildfire among youth leaders all over the globe. The story was likely retold in at least ten languages. There is now a glint of hope that volunteering with youth does not have to mean constant defeat by way of pranks. However, there is a point of contention that Stephen held over Dave for years every time that story was told. When Stephen came up out of the bed, he kicked his trombone, denting the slide, and it had to be repaired. In war, this is referred to as collateral damage, but repairs were easily made—and I think Dave might have even paid for that repair.*

STEPHEN:

Yeah, he broke my trombone.

MEMOIR NARRATION (DANA): *It was a super small price for Dave to pay in exchange for an epic story that would deliver hope to every youth leader on the planet. It is unknown to me how Dave repaid the final debt in this ultimate prank of all time—that is, the debt to Lynn who leaked and assisted in this escapade.*

STEPHEN:

Man, that was a lot of fun talking about pranks. Except for that last story. He broke my trombone.

DANA:

Well, those are casualties of war. But coming up are some times that you are going to love!

STEPHEN:

Camp? Are we finally going to camp?

DANA:

Yup, let's get to Living Waters!

STEPHEN:

Saweet!

End of Scene 6

END OF ACT I

ACT II

The Campfire Years.

"Is that a cow?!" – Beetle

Scene 7: Invitation to Camp

MEMOIR NARRATION (DANA): In the late winter and early spring of 1988, Dave began asking me if I would volunteer at Living Waters Bible Camp. He kept asking me, Stephen, and another friend of ours, Scott. Over and over, like a broken record, he just kept asking if we would give our summer to the Lord.

DAVE:

Look guys, it's a great place to be for the summer and you'd be serving God in it.

DANA:

Yeah, but the whole summer? What would I be doing?

DAVE (with a convincing smile):

Well, you'd be on the boys' staff and working on various things like mowing, trimming, stuff like that.

DANA:

But the WHOLE summer?

MEMOIR NARRATION (DANA): Now, I had been to Living Waters Bible Camp a couple years in a row as a camper, so I kinda knew what it is like to be a camper, but to be a volunteer and be a volunteer for an entire summer? What on earth would that look like? Would it be like hard labor? Like being chained to a metal ball and picking rocks? I wondered.

My wondering eventually got some answers, especially about the rocks, but that comes in a bit. Stephen, to this point, had never been to Living Waters. I would be without my friend for the summer. That would be a big deal.

Adding to my doubts, I didn't really know what it meant to give anything to the Lord. Though we all say we love God, and proclaim to be followers of Christ, how does a young person grapple with giving a significant amount of time to the unknown torment of volunteering?

A good friend of Stephen and mine, Scott, had pretty much made up his mind that he was going to try it out. But me?

DAVE:

So, what do you think?

DANA:

I'm not going unless Stephen is going.

DAVE (smiling):

Well, ok.

MEMOIR NARRATION (DANA): *Dave now knew how to lock in a two-for-one deal like a bargain shopper. It cut down his efforts and then he just needed to convince Stephen to go to camp. After a few weeks, Stephen agreed and therefore, I agreed by proxy.*

DANA:

Stephen, Dave says you are going to camp. Is that true?

STEPHEN:

Yeah, I guess so. I mean, he said if I go, you'd go.

DANA:

Well, I guess if you're going that means I'm going too!

STEPHEN:

He said you'd say something like that!

DANA (to audience):

That Stephen even agrees to go to camp is a big deal. Each summer his family vacations in Greenville, on Moosehead Lake, and he loves going to the camp on the lake. He will be on a different lake, without his family, but he does make the commitment.

STEPHEN (to audience):

Yeah, going to Moosehead Lake is the best part of my summer until this point. Neither Dana or me really know what we are getting into.

DANA (continuing):

In some ways we are ready to try something new and there is something enticing about Dave's proposal.

STEPHEN:

But in another way, we feel tricked. I'm not terribly excited about giving up my time at Moosehead Lake.

MEMOIR NARRATION (DANA): *Once we received the camp's packing list and after we shopped together, we packed our things in footlockers, grabbed our fishing poles, and hopped on a big blue church bus headed to some unknown territory where people had probably just settled a few years prior, Weston, Maine.*

MEMOIR NARRATION (Stephen joins in to the audience): *If you didn't know, there are two distinct Maines. Southern Maine is where all these city folk hang out. Northern Maine is full of woods and lumberjacks. All the men look like Paul Bunyan. I'm dead serious. They carry chainsaws and axes wherever they go. Ok, maybe that's an exaggeration.*

BACK TO DANA:

It is true that north of Bangor are trees, and lots of them. You drive about 40 miles north of Bangor with trees and more trees until getting off at exit 45 to go through Lincoln on the way to Living Waters. Well, it was exit 45 back then, before they changed the numbering to match the mileage markers. Tuck '45' into your memory, it will return later. Then, you drive through more and more woods and through a sketchy road called 169, which had claimed many an oil pan and transmission.

One frost heave would eventually get the name Coralie's Catapult, named after Coralie Duttweiler. It was a deadly piece of road that claimed the oil pan of Roger and Coralie's small economy car, that left a stream of oil that led back to the scene of the crime and a completely dry engine by the time she arrived 100 miles later in Bangor. That engine was claimed by 169 that fateful winter day.

Finally, we arrived at Living Waters. Let's take the story there.

End of Scene 7

Scene 8: Beetle Is Born

STAGE LIGHTS: Lights up.

STAGE ACTION: STEPHEN, SCOTT, and DANA hop off the bus with fishing poles in hand.

MEMOIR NARRATION (DANA): We didn't know a soul other than Dave, who would soon be leaving us, along with two or three other people from Woolwich Wiscasset Baptist Church to join the 40-50 other camp staff.

MEMOIR NARRATION (DANA, to the audience): Soon after arriving at camp, we meet a man named Ty Hutchins. Now Ty has a booming voice and laughter. His voice travels all throughout camp, extending into Butter-field Landing (where camp is located) and perhaps even traveling across the water into Canada, easily identifying Ty's location like a GPS in today's world. Note: When I say his voice entered Canada, let's be clear, even Ty Hutchins' voice still has to stop by the Canadian border crossing and check in.

STAGE ACTION: TY HUTCHINS enters, looking intently at people, like the Eye of Mordor, scouring the details from one's soul and then when ready, pops out a nickname for all to hear.

TY HUTCHINS (with a laugh looking at SCOTT, STE-PHEN and DANA):

Hey! Look! It's the three musketeers!

MEMOIR NARRATION (DANA, to the audience): One after an-other, nicknames are latching onto people. Some permanently, some temporarily. All this is happening while we stand around waiting for supper.

TY (looking right at DANA):

CRASH!

DANA:

Why Crash?

TY:

Cuz you look like you were dropped on your head!

TY (a loud laugh):

HA!

MEMOIR NARRATION (DANA, to the audience): *His eyes scour us while the gears of his brain keep working.*

TY (looking right at SCOTT):

Pee Wee!

MEMOIR NARRATION (DANA): *Now, our theater of the mind came to a screeching halt, like the needle of a record player being pulled off the vinyl recording of Ty's voice as "Pee Wee!" hangs in the air.*

I'm going to tell you right now… this wasn't going to go well… at least that is what I was thinking at the time. Scott was conscientious about his height, barely being five foot tall at the time and Scott was furious at Ty's nickname for him.

Luckily for me, Crash doesn't stick. Unfortunately for Scott, Pee Wee does, at least for a while. It eventually didn't bother him as much as it did at first because he mostly ignored it. If someone said it, he just didn't respond. Eventually, people just called him Scott again.

Placing the needle back on the record, let's get back to the story.

SCOTT (furious and red-faced):

What!? PEEWEE! NO!

TY

Oh yea, Pee Wee it is! Cuz' of your height.

TY (looking right at STEPHEN):

Beetle! That's an easy one since your last name is Bailey.

MEMOIR NARRATION (DANA, to audience): *Ty laughed again. STEPHEN grinned and readily received the nickname, but he didn't know how permanent it would be.*

STAGE ACTION: ROGER BLACK, quickly makes an entrance on the stage, halting everything in a gruff voice.

ROGER BLACK:

Whoa, wait just a minute!

DANA:

Uh, Roger? Where'd you come from?

MEMOIR NARRATION (DANA, to audience): *Roger was Assistant Director at Living Waters when Beetle and I started and became Executive Director a couple years later.*

ROGER (interrupting and pointing at TY):

Now, I gave Stephen the name Beetle!

TY (standing up):

Oh no you didn't!

MEMOIR NARRATION (DANA, to audience): *Ty is much larger than Roger. His stance looks as if there's going to be a fight.*

DANA (to audience, stepping forward):

You need not worry. This is normal. When we encounter people that are 'larger than life,' sometimes we just get a little emotional about the details. I'm sure this will settle down.

ROGER: Ty, now look, I named him Beetle soon after he got to camp.

TY:

So did I, Dana's my witness.

ROGER:

Oh no you don't, he's my witness.

DANA (turning to face both):

Now... Roger and Ty, I do clearly remember Stephen being named Beetle by Ty while we were hanging out around the front of the dining hall waiting for a meal. However... could it be that you are both right? Couldn't it be that being that his last name is Bailey, that you both latched onto the name, 'Beetle,' without giving it another thought?

TY & ROGER (in embarrassed agreement):

I guess so.

DANA (to audience):

So, Ty and Roger both claimed they named him Beetle. But you tell me — who do you think got it right?

BEETLE (pointing to audience, grinning):

Yeah, let's do this. If you think Ty named me, raise your hand.

STAGE ACTION: AUDIENCE reacts, DANA counts hands.

BEETLE:

And if you think Roger named me, raise your hand.

STAGE ACTION: AUDIENCE reacts.

DANA (smiling):

See? Still no consensus. I guess Beetle just... named himself.

STAGE ACTION: The AUDIENCE chuckles.

DANA (to audience):

Phew, crisis averted.

STAGE ACTION: DANA wipes his brow. ROGER and TY exit the stage.

MEMOIR NARRATION (DANA): *From the days, weeks, and months to follow, Beetle was cemented into Stephen's being, forged together as one in the hot flames of Ty, the nickname blacksmith. Stephen became Beetle, due to Ty Hutchins, and is likely the single most significant nickname forged by his fires of Ty that would stand the test of time.*

Beetle launches forward and our camp life is launched like a rocket into the unknown, never to return to its point of origin.

Forty-five

MEMOIR NARRATION (DANA, to audience): *Someone at camp approached BEETLE.*

CAMPER:

Beetle, how old are you?

BEETLE:

45.

CAMPER:

Really, 45?

BEETLE (without even cracking a smile):

Yup.

DANA:

Why did you tell that kid you are 45?

BEETLE:

I don't know, it was the first thing that came to my head.

MEMOIR NARRATION (DANA): *45 was born that day. Some would say, "I can't believe you are 45?" Or, "You don't look 45." But Beetle would just say, "yup."*

Now, one might wonder, "What happens on his birthday?"

BEETLE

45.

MEMOIR NARRATION (DANA): *It was appropriate that the exit to Lincoln was numbered as "45" as you take that exit to find, 45, that is, Beetle.*

BEETLE

Hey 45! That's my age!

MEMOIR NARRATION (DANA, to audience): *Yup, he says that every time he sees the number 45.*

Rocks and More Rocks

MEMOIR NARRATION (DANA): *Remember what I said about camp and the fear of never-ending manual labor? Well, my nightmare came true. Yet, at the same time a pivotal shift occurred in how I viewed my best friend, Stephen, henceforth to be referred to as Beetle.*

Having never really been engaged in any more than a few hours of volunteering with Beetle, volunteering hour after hour, day after day, week after week, showed me that Beetle truly could find humor in anything. He could turn the worst situation into the best.

You know the phrase about turning lemons into lemonade? Beetle turned lemons into lemonade, lemon squares, lemon meringue pie, lemon cheesecake, and the list keeps going. He became a machine for humor, except you don't even need to put coins in. Just be around the laughing machine and "funny" just seems to happen. No matter the situation, it always went to lighthearted humor with Beetle that still got the job done and took the sting out of every difficulty.

STAGE ACTION: The lower driveway of Living Waters with wheelbarrows and rocks. BEETLE, DANA, and other BOY STAFF working.

STAGE ACTION: ROGER AND MIKE (THE HEAD OF BOY STAFF) give the boy staff some instruction.

MEMOIR NARRATION (DANA): Our first task at camp was to work on the driveway that led to the newly built Med Wry chapel, built in memory of evangelist Med Wry. The driveway was full of rocks. Ugh. Unscreened gravel that was used to create the driveway might have saved a few bucks, but cost us a lot of time in hard labor.

ROGER BLACK (standing in the long gravel driveway):

Boys, here you got rakes, you got shovels, you got wheelbarrows. We need all these rocks picked up and leave just the gravel.

MIKE PHILLIPS (holding up a small stone):

If it is a rock any bigger than this, it's gotta go.

ROGER (hopping on a three-wheeler):

We are going to keep coming by and checking on your progress.

SOUND EFFECT: VROOM.

STAGE ACTION: ROGER is off to check on other projects.

DANA (swallowing hard):

Ugh. Manual labor. I was right.

BEETLE:

Whelp. Let's get it done!

SOUND EFFECT: Variety of protests.

STAFF GUYS (one at a time):

This is crazy!

Man, look at all these rocks!

I had no idea camp would be like this.

BEETLE (determined):

Ain't gonna do no good complaining, boys, we got a job to do, let's do it.

MEMOIR NARRATION (DANA): *Have you ever been involved in a job that when you close your eyes, it is all you see? We see rocks. We dream rocks. We taste rocks. Join back with us now at the lower driveway of Living Waters. It was now day two of hard labor on a driveway which will eventually house a new RV park area and lead to the newly built Med Wry chapel on the lower side of camp.*

SOUND EFFECT: CLUNK, CLUNK… *The sounds of the rocks as we drop them into wheelbarrows.*

DANA:

Man, this is hard work.

BOYS' STAFF MEMBER:

How long do we have to do this?

BEETLE:

Until it's done, they say. This is our only job until it's done.

MEMOIR NARRATION (DANA, to audience): *The rocks were of all different sizes, some smaller, some larger, most seem around five pounds.*

BEETLE:

Guys, get to work, here comes Roger.

SOUND EFFECT: Fading VROOM of a three-wheeler

STAGE ACTION: ROGER BLACK speeds in on a three-wheeler with his thinning hair flapping in the wind. He stops right where we are working.

ROGER:

How's it going boys?

STAFF GUY:

How long do we gotta do this?

ROGER:

Until it's done. We gotta get this driveway ready as camper sites. Keep it up, looking good. Get it done.

SOUND EFFECT: Fading VROOM of a three-wheeler

MEMOIR NARRATION (DANA, to audience): He's off again. We go back to work, taking breaks by leaning on our rakes on the sweltering June day.

MEMOIR NARRATION (DANA): Blisters are something we hadn't accounted for when we ran through the logic of making a commitment to camp.

Scott developed some pretty good blisters that day. Note: I never called him Pee Wee.

WENDELL CALDER, the Director, stops by to check on progress (his gray "preacher hair" perfectly groomed as always).

WENDELL (in his raspy preacher voice):

Hmm. It needs more work boys. You aren't off this task until it's done.

STAGE ACTION: WENDELL walks off.

SOUND EFFECT: WHOMP WHOMP. *A long and low sound comes from the bog next to where we are working.*

MEMOIR NARRATION (DANA, to audience): *Let's give a name to one of our staff guys that summer. That name: Danny Jack.*

DANNY JACK:

Is that a cow?

SOUND EFFECT: Laughter from stage and audience.

MEMOIR NARRATION (DANA): *Being from West Virginia, DANNY apparently had never heard a Maine bullfrog before.*

Beetle, the ultimate humorist, equipped with Danny Jack's words as raw material, began to fuel comedy that everyone wanted to get in on. Beetle could be straight-faced and serious as a heart attack about anything.

BEETLE:

Is that a cow? No! It's a bullfrog.

BEETLE (continuing):

Cow's go, "MOOOOoooo!" Frogs go, "WHOMP WHOMP!"

MEMOIR NARRATION (DANA, to audience): *DANNY is embarrassed.*

Every time we hear a bullfrog:

BEETLE

Is that a cow?

MEMOIR NARRATION (DANA, to audience): *With an absolutely serious face. Time after time. Laughter after laughter.*

STAGE ACTION: *Then BEETLE starts changing the intonation to make it more interesting, emphasizing different words.*

BEETLE

IS that a cow?

MEMOIR NARRATION (DANA, to audience): Then

BEETLE

Is THAT a cow?

BEETLE

Is that A cow?

MEMOIR NARRATION (DANA, to audience): Finally

BEETLE

Is that a COW!?

MEMOIR NARRATION (DANA): His keeping us in stitches that day helped us all push through the challenge.

Events like that make working a joy instead of a chore and this turns into a series of long-running jokes for Beetle. He occasionally threw out, "Is that a cow?", no matter where we were or what we were doing and all of the boy's staff would crack up again. I truly hope that Danny does not have any resentment toward Beetle for his sense of humor. That first year at camp brought us many long-running jokes.

Day after day for about 1,000 days we worked on that driveway. Ok, really, it was just four days, but the time flies by with Beetle.

Puke Luke

STAGE ACTION: *SPLIT LEFT – Dana's dorm with BRUCE BEALS. SPLIT RIGHT – Beetle's dorm with JEREMY BLACK and MIKE PHILLIPS.*

MEMOIR NARRATION (DANA): I was in a dorm with a counselor named Bruce Beals and right next to my dorm was Beetle, Jeremy Black (the Assistant Director's son), and Mike Phillips, the leader of the boy's staff that *summer. Beetle's dorm wasn't a "camper dorm," it was just staff. My room, with a counselor, would house kids each week.*

Each evening, without fail, I heard something going on in the dorm next to us when it was time for "lights out!" It went something like this. Let's jump back into the scene.

STAGE ACTION: *DANA is laying in his top bunk next to the wall of Beetle's dorm.*

MIKE:

Ok, boys, I know you know there's time for horsing around and time to be serious. This is time to be serious. I'm going to turn the lights out and I don't want to hear anything from you guys.

STAGE ACTION: MIKE flips off the light switch and the crack of light in the dorm wall that DANA can see from his dorm flicks out.

A few seconds pass.

JEREMY (low voice):

Puke Luke.

MEMOIR NARRATION (DANA, to audience): *Immediately MIKE jumps out of bed.*

MIKE:

Ohhh, I wish you hadn't said that!

MEMOIR NARRATION (DANA, to audience): *With a flick, the crack of light through the dorm wall comes back on.*

MIKE:

How many times have I told you to NEVER call me Puke Luke! I'm gonna get you tonight.

JEREMY:

No, ahh, ahh, no, no, I give up, I GIVE UP!

MIKE:

You gonna say it again?

JEREMY:

No, no, I promise, you aren't a Puke Luke, I take it back.

MEMOIR NARRATION (DANA, to audience): *JEREMY sighs as if getting some relief. BEETLE can be heard laughing away in the background.*

MIKE:

Alright, boys, there's time for horsin' around and there's time to be serious. This is time to be serious. I'm gonna flip this light off and I don't want to hear a thing.

SOUND EFFECT: SNAP!

MEMOIR NARRATION (DANA, to audience): *The crack of light goes out again.*

JEREMY (soft voice):

Puke Luke.

MIKE:

That's it, I knew you couldn't be trusted.

MEMOIR NARRATION (DANA, to audience): *MIKE flies out of his bunk.*

SOUND EFFECT: SNAP!

MEMOIR NARRATION (DANA, to audience): The light is on again. This might have happened 4 or 5 times each night and every time was as funny as the first.

Now, Beetle, being much larger than Mike, could pull a "Puke Luke" without any significant repercussions. There could be some camp mythology or folklore that leads us to the origins of "Puke Luke," but it is mostly unknown.

DANA:

Beetle, can we pause on camp for a few minutes and just talk about your life skills?

BEETLE:

Oh, I guess so. But we are going to get back to camp, right?

DANA:

I promise.

End of Scene 8

Scene 9: A Life Full of Skills

STAGE ACTION: A series of small tableaux across the stage. Each spotlight reveals BEETLE in a different "skill station" with props. DANA introduces each briefly, then steps aside while Beetle or a prop-driven gag carries the moment.

Opening

DANA (to audience):

Beetle was a man of many skills — humble, funny, and never the one to brag. Let's take a look.

Tableau 1 – The Tinker

STAGE LIGHTS: Spotlight on the workbench with broken radio, toolbox.

BEETLE (fiddling with screws, muttering to himself):

C'mon now, just a twist here… hey, it works!

PROPS: Broken appliance lights up or sparks.

DANA (aside, chuckling):

His dad called him "Tinker." Only his dad was allowed.

Tableau 2 – The Music Lover

STAGE LIGHTS: Spotlight on BEETLE with a boom box, holding a Petra cassette.

BEETLE (shouting over the music):

Yeah, Dana, Bryan Duncan's the best! "I've got this lunatic friend!"

BEETLE & DANA (belt the chorus, grinning at each other):

I've got this LUNATIC FRIEND!

SOUND EFFECT: Crowd laughs.

DANA (aside):

He never puffed himself up — but man, he knew his music.

Tableau 3 – The Trombone Player

STAGE LIGHTS: Spotlight on BEETLE with a trombone.

GINA ANDERSON (enters, piano music in background):

Remember how they'd ruin the last note of rehearsal just to make us laugh?

BEETLE (sliding trombone wrong note — sour sound)

Oops.

SOUND EFFECT: Crowd laughs.

GINA (smiling at audience):

They were jokers, but good musicians. Crisp, on time… and mostly on key.

Tableau 4 – The Singer

STAGE LIGHTS: Spotlight on BEETLE with microphone.

BEETLE (bashfully, then belting one line):

♪ The Road to Zion in your heart… ♪

DANA (applauding):

He had a voice that filled a room, though he'd shrug it off every time.

Tableau 5 – Games & Skip-Bo

STAGE LIGHTS: Spotlight on the table with cards. KIMBERLY sits across from BEETLE.

KIMBERLY (frustrated, slamming cards):

Stephen! You HAVE to be cheating!

BEETLE (to audience, whispering, poker face):

Hey, Skip-Bo rules… out-of-turn play counts if no one notices.

KIMBERLY (groaning):

Ugh!

SOUND EFFECT: Laughter.

Tableau 6 – Balderdash

STAGE LIGHTS: Spotlight on the family dining table. Cards in hand.

DANA'S MOM (struggling not to laugh):

The word is SOSS, let's see what this definition says, "It's Morse Code for help… the guy started a second time but was shot and couldn't finish."

BEETLE (straight-faced):

Totally legit definition.

SOUND EFFECT: WHOLE TABLE bursts in laughter.

Tableau 7 – Puzzles & Rubik's Cube

STAGE LIGHTS: Spotlight on Beetle with Rubik's Cube.

BEETLE (spins cube, snaps last piece into place):

Well, it's just three formulas. Easy.

STAGE ACTION: BEETLE tosses a cube to a kid in the audience.

Tableau 8 – Treasure Hunting

STAGE LIGHTS: Spotlight on Beetle with metal detector, headphones.

SOUND EFFECT: Beep-beep-beep.

BEETLE (excited):

Gold! …Oh. Just a rusty spoon.

Tableau 9 – Pets

STAGE LIGHTS: Spotlight on BEETLE with a leash, holding invisible "Max."

BEETLE (to audience):

This is Max. Rotten dog. Rotten! Worst punk of a dog I ever owned.

BEETLE (softly):

…but I loved him.

Closing

DANA (to audience)

See? Tinker, musician, singer, gamer, puzzle-solver, treasure-hunter, animal-lover. Beetle never bragged, but his life was full of skills — and plenty of laughter.

End of Scene 9

Scene 10: Finishing Up That First Year of Camp

MEMOIR NARRATION (DANA, to audience): By the time our first year at camp comes to a close, Beetle has taken center stage in the hearts of many. He can't hardly go anywhere without hearing someone call out, "Beetle!"

Beetle's nickname has been cemented solidly into his being, which can be witnessed in the following account. Beetle's dad and mom, Jimmy and Lynn, drive into camp one day for a surprise visit. Jimmy rolls down his window and questions one of the staff, Lisa Elliott who recalls this story.

STAGE ACTION: A sedan pulls up and the driver's window rolls down.

JIMMY:

Do you know where I can find Stephen Bailey?

MEMOIR NARRATION (DANA, to audience): LISA, who knows most everyone at camp, has to think for a minute.

LISA (puzzled):

I don't think we have anyone here by that name… Oh, Beetle!

MEMOIR NARRATION (DANA, to audience): Already, few recognize Beetle by the name of Stephen. Lisa, and some others, affectionately call Jimmy and Lynn as "Mr. and Mrs. Beetle," which they too wear as a badge of honor.

In fact, we start hearing the name, "Beetle!" called out just about everywhere. He gets the nickname at Living Waters by Ty Hutchins, but since so many people come in and out of camp the name "Beetle" travels across the state and eventually, the country. It travels being carried by the memories of adults, campers, and staff.

VOICE FROM BACK OF THE THEATER

Hey, Beetle!

BEETLE (responds):

Hey, what's going on?

MEMOIR NARRATION (DANA, to audience): *People see him 30 miles away in Houlton.*

ANOTHER VOICE

Hey, Beetle!

BEETLE:

Hey, what's going on?

MEMOIR NARRATION (DANA, to audience): *Then we see people 100 miles away in Bangor.*

YET ANOTHER VOICE

Hey, Beetle!

BEETLE:

Hey, what's going on?

MEMOIR NARRATION (DANA, to audience): *Then we are on road trips much later in life and see people at random in other states.*

MEMOIR NARRATION: DANA, to audience): *The nickname is more than a nickname for some small sliver in time, no, it is welded onto this 17-year old like a metal badge. He wears that badge with pride.*

That year brings us life-long friends. For me, and I promised I would get back to this, I met a wonderful girl named Angela Perkins. I am sixteen at this time and she is fourteen. We didn't know it then, but we will get married after a 5-year long-distance relationship (seeing each other mostly at camp, then writing lots and lots of letters when we are away from each other). Eventually we have two children, Caleb and Aaron.

Beetle comes away from camp with loads of friends. One is particularly close. Amanda. She is a super happy girl that loves hearing stories, hanging out with

Beetle, and is probably the first voice standing above the fray that calls out, "Beetle!" with a warm tone and a smile anytime that Beetle is in proximity. Amanda captures Beetle's heart.

You can see that Beetle has a warm smile right now when hearing the name, "Amanda," she will also be one of many that makes a final trek to see Beetle in his last days. Next to my family, living in North Carolina, when Beetle passes, Amanda travels the furthest to see her camp-time buddy.

At the end of the summer of 1988, we said good bye to our camp family, got back on the big blue bus from WWBC and headed home.

That blue bus is no longer just a form of transportation, it is like a special invention that brings us to a place and a time where all things would change. It is as if it has a magic power to change people by taking them to a stop on life's journey where experiences would be made that would change a person from the inside.

Only God can do that. The bus itself, I know, isn't special. Camp is special. It is because we come with a willingness to serve God, that God does something special in our lives. As we get on the bus that August day of 1988, we leave something at camp and we will need to return back to explore more. It is like the ultimate treasure hunt.

As we consider Beetle's kind-hearted spirit and his capacity to serve in challenging situations, we must identify strong sources of training and examples. Various people in particular show exceptional kindness to Beetle and exemplify limitless servitude that we also see in Beetle. These, I believe, are foundational relationships that should not be overlooked in Beetle's story.

Reverend Wendell and Joan Calder

MEMOIR NARRATION (DANA, to audience): God used the Calders to help establish Living Waters Bible Camp to reach young and old with the gospel of Jesus Christ. Wendell Calder was the director during our early years of service at the camp.

STAGE LIGHTS: *A glow increases on the stage next to BEETLE. WEN-DELL CALDER with his perfectly groomed gray hair, polo shirt, and slacks becomes apparent.*

WENDELL:

Beetle, I remember I asked you if you washed your hands, and you said, 'Of course, right before I went to the bathroom.'

BEETLE:

Well, yeah, isn't that when you are supposed to wash your hands?

WENDELL (to Beetle):

Whenever the camp needed anything, you were willing. I thank you for that and I thank God for your service.

Roger and Karen Black

MEMOIR NARRATION (DANA): *In our earlier years at camp, Roger Black was Assistant Director. Roger was a perfect example of giving under all situations. His wife Karen was like a mother when our real mothers aren't around. Hundreds of stories could probably be told about Roger and Karen and their service, probably even thousands.*

Those of us planted in the soil of Living Waters as servants of Christ had the perfect opportunity to learn, grow, and serve. It was as if we were little plants in the greenhouse with caretakers watching over us.

With camp over for the summer, we returned to school. Beetle was a senior, I was a junior. Our lives were changed forever.

Scott, Beetle, and I constantly spoke of our camp experiences pretty much every day. It carried us into the next summer where our camp experiences would continue. The barrier to us, like a brick wall, was the school year and we just waited with anticipation to escape the drudgery of reading, writing, and arithmetic, so we could get reconnected.

Each year at camp would prove to be different. Some faces would return, some would be replaced with new faces. Certain people would be like water, soil, and sunshine to Beetle, myself, and many others.

Reflective Monologue

(A *monologue* is a speech delivered by a single character, offering insight, story, or emotion directly to the audience.)

STAGE LIGHTS: Spotlight on DANA, stepping forward, addressing the audience.

MEMOIR NARRATION (DANA, reflective): *That first summer at camp changed everything. We had gone in as kids, full of doubts, mischief, and a love for fun. But by the end of that summer of 1988, something deeper had taken root. Camp wasn't just a place to work or a way to fill our days — it was where faith became real. It was where friendships grew into family, where joy was forged even in blisters and long hours, and where Beetle found his name and, I believe, his calling.*

When we boarded that bus home, we carried more than fishing poles and tired bodies. We carried the beginning of lifelong bonds, the shaping of who we would become, and the assurance that God had used that summer to mark us forever.

MEMOIR NARRATION (DANA, pausing, with a smile): *We didn't just leave camp behind that August. Camp stayed with us — in our laughter, in our friendships, and in every choice that followed.*

STAGE LIGHTS: Lights dim. End of scene.

End of Scene 10

Scene 11: The Guidance Counselor

DANA:

I suggest we talk about school.

BEETLE (with disgust):

Gross-atosis. BLUCK!

MEMOIR NARRATION (DANA): Beetle isn't especially gifted at complying with the traditional education system. His method of learning and retaining information worked differently than most. He was a genius in many ways, seeing through the flawed system and hating assignments that were designed to keep students busy rather than teaching them something. He'd rather be building rockets, working in the school's auto shop, woodshop, or making music than being cooped up in school.

As mentioned before, his memory is excellent. He could hear something once in class and do well on tests.

BEETLE (interrupting and disgusted):

Funny isn't it? Tests are supposed to measure knowledge, right? So why all the stinkin' homework if you do well on the tests?

MEMOIR NARRATION (DANA): While Beetle may have been slow at writing and reading, with his exceptional memory, he didn't really need to be fast at those things.

DANA:

Beetle, we need to cover this part of your story. People should know about it.

BEETLE:

Okay, I'll tell it myself then. I hated school. Every bit of it. What's the point if you know the material and can memorize things, but teachers give you assignments for those who DON'T know it instead of those who DO? It's crazy. It's stupid.

STAGE ACTION: The GUIDANCE COUNSELOR enters and sits behind her desk, looking at BEETLE with concern.

COUNSELOR:

Stephen, you need to think about your future. What are you going to do? What are you going to be?

BEETLE:

I'm going to work at camp. I'm going to live in Danforth.

COUNSELOR (puzzled):

Going to camp? How will that bring you any income?

BEETLE:

I don't know, but I'm going to go work at camp and I'm going to live in Danforth.

COUNSELOR:

Now, Stephen, that's no way to live. You have so many talents and abilities. Haven't you thought about college?

BEETLE:

Nope. I ain't going to college. I'm going to work at camp and I'm going to live in Danforth.

COUNSELOR:

Maybe vocational college?

BEETLE (voice rising):

NO! You don't get it. I'm going to go to work at camp and I'm going to live in Danforth and that's it.

MEMOIR NARRATION (DANA): *And that is exactly what happened.*

Now, I will say in the counselor's defense that she was likely doing her job, but she clearly had no idea what camp and the Danforth area meant to Beetle. Let me explain something important about what was happening for Beetle.

While the guidance counselor remained puzzled about Beetle's decision to go to camp and eventually move to Danforth, something else was happening. Beetle was getting an education, but it was incompatible with the kind of education that institutions are designed to produce.

At the same time Beetle was failing his senior year in high school, he was on track to earn a doctorate degree in servitude.

DANA:

How does Doctor Beetle sound to you?

BEETLE (with disgust):

Bluck!

MEMOIR NARRATION (DANA): *The course of humankind and the course of the kingdom of God are two incompatible paths. In Ephesians 2:1-10, Paul explains this clearly.*

Beetle avoided a decision that would have put him on track to follow the passions of the flesh and carry out the desires of the body and mind by committing early to what he believed God wanted him to do. Just like his new name, Beetle had cemented into himself that God would use him at Living Waters and Danforth, and he would pursue that calling, even unto death.

When Beetle makes up his mind due to conviction, that's final. There's no changing it or convincing him otherwise. This is especially true about Beetle's salvation. So many people make a decision to follow the Lord, then waver. There was never any wavering for Beetle. He made up his mind that Jesus loved him and he trusted

Jesus as his savior. That settled it in Beetle's mind, even though he made this decision as a young boy.

That first year at camp added a new layer to Beetle. It gave him knowledge that he could push through the unknown, and that humor could be a sword he could carry everywhere to diffuse hard situations. It was a sword he wielded well.

Beetle failed his senior year. It was devastating, but it did put us both into the same graduating year (though at two different schools).

BEETLE:

And miss camp? No way! If I went to summer school it would be the most miserable summer of my life!

I went to camp and my good buddy Dana's mother helped me graduate in '90 instead of '89.

MEMOIR NARRATION (DANA): *I came home many times from school to find Beetle sitting at my kitchen table with my mother going through English or some other failed subject.*

Beetle's confidence grew. He knew he had a gift for making people laugh, but what he really needed right then was to pass high school!

With help from my mom, who got to know Beetle on a whole new level, and through many laughs, she helped him pass his overdue classes and graduate. Beetle didn't walk at graduation - he felt like his class, the class of 1989, was his real class.

It's too bad he never really reconnected much with any of his classmates and never attended a reunion, but honestly, he didn't have many friends at school that I knew of. Most of his friends were connections from WWBC or camp.

In appreciation for my mom, Beetle made something in shop class. He called me on the phone.

BEETLE:

Hey Dana, I'm gonna come over and measure something.

DANA:

Yeah, sure.

BEETLE:

I want to make something for your mother. She's helped so much this year.

DANA:

What are you gonna make?

STAGE LIGHTS: Spotlight shines on a tall object covered by a blanket.

MEMOIR NARRATION (DANA, to audience): Beetle gets up from his stool and walks over to it.

BEETLE:

I made this!

MEMOIR NARRATION (DANA, to audience): Beetle whips off the blanket and uncovers a beautiful corner hutch.

DANA:

WOW! Mom is going to LOVE it!

MEMOIR NARRATION (DANA): He created a wonderful corner hutch that hangs on my parents' dining room wall to this day. Beetle isn't one for crafting verbal 'thank yous', but he certainly knows how to build a tangible form of his gratitude. This "thank you" brought tears to my mom's eyes.

End of Scene 11

END OF ACT II

ACT III
The Turning Point.

"Here you go, now we're even!" – Beetle

Scene 12: Camp Days Continue

Opening

***MEMOIR NARRATION (DANA,* to audience**): *The summer of 1989 brought more humor, more hard work, and more memories than we could count. Let me show you just a few…*

Vignette 1 – Dump Run ("Disneyland")

STAGE ACTION: BEETLE drives an imaginary camp truck. DANA rides shotgun. A few STAFF KIDS in back.

BEETLE (calling out, dead serious):

Who wants to go to the dump? …

MEMOIR NARRATION (DANA): *Silence hung in the air.*

BEETLE (grinning):

Alright, who wants to go to DISNEYLAND!?

STAFF KIDS (cheering, hands raised):

Me! Me! Me!

STAGE ACTION: STAFF KIDS pile in and the truck rattles off.

SOUND EFFECT: Audience laughs.

Vignette 2 – Skit Night

STAGE ACTION: Camp tabernacle, chairs in rows, African drumbeat in background. BEETLE stands center stage, spinning a long-winded tale.

MEMOIR NARRATION (DANA): *Let's make this brief. In reality, Beetle droned on and on about how to catch a pink elephant. The audience at Skit Night endured it, patiently hoping and waiting for a punch line. Finally, Beetle finished up with…*

BEETLE (dramatic voice):

So the pink elephant got so mad that it huffed and puffed and stomped its feed until it turned blue! Then you go home, 'cuz anybody and their brother can catch a blue elephant.

SOUND EFFECT: AUDIENCE groaning, laughing, and clapping.

BEETLE:

See, Dana, they're clapping.

DANA (aside, chuckling):

Yeah, because it's OVER!

Vignette 3 – Walking to Million Dollar View

MEMOIR NARRATION (DANA): *At the time, the Million Dollar View was a restaurant in Weston, Maine, on top of a hill and we would walk there almost each Saturday to buy supper and hang out.*

STAGE ACTION: A GROUP OF FRIENDS walking on a trail.

SOUND EFFECT: Whomp, whomp of a frog.

BEETLE:

Is that a COW?

STAGE ACTION: Everyone laughs.

DANA:

You ain't ever gonna let Danny live that down, are you?

BEETLE:

Nope!

Vignette 4 – Deep Friendships

STAGE LIGHTS: Spotlight on DANA and ANGELA sitting together.

STAGE ACTION: BEETLE and AMANDA laugh in the background, skipping stones.

DANA (to audience, quietly, memoir voice):

These weren't just camp friends anymore. They were the ones we'd carry in our lives for years to come.

Closing

DANA (stepping forward, reflective)

Work, laughter, friendships, faith — all of it came together that summer. And it wasn't just camp anymore. It was home.

STAGE LIGHTS: Lights dim. End of scene.

End of Scene 12

Scene 13: Life is Changing

STAGE LIGHTS: Heavenly glow.

GOD:

Have you considered my servant Beetle? How he laughs and has such good humor.

SATAN (hissing):

That's only because you've allowed him and Dana to be together.

GOD:

Yes, they are good friends.

SATAN:

Allow me to separate them for a few years and you'll see—Beetle won't be that funny or bring joy.

GOD:

Ok, but I will set the boundaries. Do as you say, but only that. Don't touch their summers.

STAGE LIGHTS: Spotlight fades. Curtains close.

Monologue 1 – Dana pacing in front of curtain

STAGE ACTION: DANA rubs his palms nervously, miming a tie straightening. Paces the stage, addressing the audience directly.

DANA (to audience):

Months earlier, I had taken a trip to Alexander, Maine. Sat in Ed and Janet's living room—nerves of jelly. Janet's in the kitchen washing dishes. I hear Ed's car. (Mimes door opening.) He walks in, sits in his easy chair, and I think… *"I might throw up."*

STAGE ACTION: Dana wipes his forehead, breathes deep, gestures with hands like shaking.

STAGE ACTION: Curtain opens to living room. ED and JANET on stage. DANA seated nervously.

JANET (to ED walking in):

Good afternoon! Dana is in the living room and has something to talk to you about.

ED (to DANA):

Well, what brings you up here? It's a four-hour drive.

DANA (stammering):

Uh… you know your daughter and I… I want to ask for your blessing… and for her hand in marriage.

ED (leaning back, smiling gently):

Aha! What are you going to do with the rest of her?

STAGE ACTION: DANA looks faint, clutches chest.

DANA:

You know what I mean.

ED (smiling kindly):

Well, Angela is old enough to make her own decisions. So, I give you my blessing.

DANA (to audience, relieved, hands to chest):

I patted myself down, just to make sure I was still alive.

STAGE ACTION: Curtain closes.

Monologue 2 – Dana during scene change

STAGE ACTION: DANA mimes counting money, writing letters.

DANA:

While working for Dave selling Christmas trees in Virginia, I pinched pennies for a ring. We wrote letters—long ones. Called after 8 PM when the rates were cheaper. Every envelope and every phone call stitched our lives closer.

STAGE ACTION: Curtain opens to Popham Beach. Cold, gray set. Bench downstage.

DANA (knells, shivering):

Angela Lynn Perkins, will you marry me?

ANGELA (tears in eyes):

Yes.

STAGE ACTION: Curtain closes on the frozen tableau of the proposal.

Monologue 3 – Audience interaction

STAGE ACTION: DANA walks forward, still trembling with excitement. He holds out his hand like a ring box is in it.

DANA:

She said yes! Not just because I had the keys to get us back into the car where it was warm, but because she loved me. We'd survived long distance, letters, late-night calls… Now, marriage. Beetle? He would be my best man!

STAGE ACTION: Pauses, scanning audience as if inviting a question.

AUDIENCE MEMBER (improv):

Why was Beetle your best man?

DANA (big smile):

Because he was my brother in spirit. Scott and Chris stood beside me, too, but Beetle? He was my lifelong friend. Oh—and we all wore cartoon socks. Hidden under our tuxes. (Lifts pant leg to mime showing socks.) Don't tell Angela.

SOUND EFFECT: Audience laughter.

AUDIENCE MEMBER (improv):

Now, I imagine Beetle pulling a good prank on your wedding vehicle… What was that like?

DANA:

Well, believe me, I had thought of that. So, what I did was put Beetle in charge of making sure the car wasn't decorated or pranked too badly. He did that job well!

SOUND EFFECT: "Ahh" in agreement and approval from the audience.

STAGE ACTION: Curtain opens to Wedding Tableau.

(A *tableau* is a staged "living picture," where actors freeze in position to capture a moment visually before action continues.)

DANA and ANGELA, BEETLE as best man, AMANDA and TRISH singing. The wedding party was frozen like a picture.

DANA (monologue, to audience):

Amanda sang. Beetle stood beside me. Scott and Chris were grooms-men. My Dad officiated the wedding. It was October 2nd, 1993. The day my life truly changed.

STAGE ACTION: Curtain closes.

Monologue 4 – Life's Transitions

STAGE ACTION: DANA pulls letters from his jacket, reads them silently, then speaks.

DANA:

Marriage brought a long separation. Angela and I moved to Virginia for Liberty University. Beetle? He went to Word of Life Bible Institute with Amanda. We kept in touch through letters and calls.

STAGE ACTION: He looks at the audience.

DANA:

Ever get that feeling when your best friend lives far away, but you can pick up right where you left off? That was Beetle.

BEETLE (from backstage, shouting):

Hey Dana, are you still boring the audience with blah blah blah? Let's get back to camp already!

DANA (rolling eyes):

You got me going… Now I gotta finish this backstory!

BEETLE (grumbling offstage):

Sheesh. You give a guy an inch…

SOUND EFFECT: Audience laughter.

STAGE ACTION: Curtain opens slowly.

Final Stage – Beetle's Prophecy Fulfilled

STAGE ACTION: ROGER, BEETLE, and DANA center stage.

ROGER:

Why don't you stay at camp year-round?

BEETLE:

And do what?

ROGER:

Help with the animals, fix things. You can earn your keep.

BEETLE (big smile):

That sounds great!

MEMOIR NARRATION (DANA, voiceover): And so Beetle's *prophecy to his counselor came true. "I'm going to work at camp and I'm going to live in Danforth."*

End of Scene 13

Scene 14: Hardship Strikes

STAGE LIGHTS: Heavenly glow.

MEMOIR NARRATION (DANA, voiceover): *In the heavens, Satan observes how God has brought together a tight-knit family despite his attempts at destruction.*

GOD:

Have you considered my servant Beetle, how he did not stop bringing joy even when you took Dana from him?

SATAN (hissing):

You've allowed them back together! But Beetle is close to his father. Let me take his father away and he will curse you.

GOD:

Go and do as you say, but only his father.

STAGE LIGHTS: Spotlight returns to earth.

STAGE ACTION: Curtain closes.

Monologue 1 – Jimmy's Death

STAGE ACTION: DANA steps forward, phone in hand.

MEMOIR NARRATION (DANA, to audience): *Beetle's dad, Jimmy, had a servant's heart. Every summer, he drove buses at Living Waters, giving his time with joy.*

STAGE ACTION: Phone to ear. DANA flinches as he hears Lynn's voice.

LYNN (on the phone):

Jimmy has passed away.

STAGE ACTION: DANA lowers phone, hand trembling.

MEMOIR NARRATION (DANA, to audience): *When Beetle returned from his wilderness trip that day, his world was different forever.*

STAGE ACTION: Curtain opens to tableau.

• BEETLE sits on a bench, elbows on knees, face in hands.

• STAFF MEMBERS stand at a respectful distance.

STAGE LIGHTS: A single spotlight isolates BEETLE.

DANA (voiceover):

He cried and cried… but never cursed God.

STAGE LIGHTS: Lights dim. Curtains close.

READER'S NOTE: *James A. "Jimmy" Bailey passed away on August 13, 2001. He was a devoted husband and father, remembered for his faithful service at Living Waters Bible Camp, especially as a bus driver during sports camps.*

(A Reader's Note is prose only [not staged]. It gives factual background for readers about time, place, and significance.)

STAGE LIGHTS: Heavenly glow.

GOD:

Have you seen anyone like my servant Beetle? You've battered him with your evil ways, yet he rejoices still.

SATAN

That's only because you've spared his younger brother. Let me take Chris, and he will curse you.

GOD

Go ahead, but only his youngest brother, Chris.

STAGE LIGHTS: Spotlight returns to earth.

STAGE ACTION: Curtain closes.

Monologue 2 – Chris's Death

STAGE ACTION: DANA holds a hospital wristband.

DANA (to audience):

Not long after Jimmy's death, Beetle's younger brother Chris suffered headaches. Cancer.

STAGE ACTION: He lowers wristband slowly.

DANA:

Surgery. Treatment. For a time, he recovered… but years later, on December 21st, 2014, we lost him.

STAGE ACTION: Curtain opens to tableau.

• CHRIS in a hospital bed, family surrounding him.

• BEETLE stands alone, looking upward.

DANA (voiceover):

Again, Beetle did not curse God. His joy returned slowly, scarred but still alive.

STAGE LIGHTS: Lights fade.

STAGE ACTION: Curtain closes.

READER'S NOTE: *Christopher A. Bailey, 42, of Woolwich, Maine, died December 21, 2014, at his mother's home in Wiscasset. He was survived by his* *daughter, Violet Lynn Bailey, his mother Madelyn, and brothers James, Mark, and Stephen (Beetle). His obituary appeared in the* Wiscasset Newspaper.

STAGE LIGHTS: Heavenly glow.

GOD:

Have you ever seen anyone resist cursing me after losing father and brother?

SATAN (hissing):

Not yet. He is close to his mother. Take her, and he will curse you.

GOD:

Go ahead, but only his mother.

STAGE LIGHTS: Spotlight returns to earth.

STAGE ACTION: Curtain closes.

Monologue 3 – Lynn's Death

STAGE ACTION: DANA holds a quilt square.

DANA (to audience):

Lynn, Beetle's mother, was fierce in her love. She sang in the choir, taught Sunday School, and spent summers serving at Living Waters.

STAGE ACTION: He holds the quilt square gently.

But Parkinson's weakened her. On November 10th, 2021, she passed away.

STAGE ACTION: Curtain opens to tableau.

• An empty rocking chair with a quilt draped over it.

- BEETLE stands beside it, head bowed.

- Soft candle-like lighting.

DANA (voiceover):

Three losses: father, brother, mother. And still Beetle did not raise his fist at God. The scars were real, but so was his faith.

STAGE LIGHTS: Lights dim to black.

STAGE ACTION: Curtain closes.

READER'S NOTE: *Madelyn L. Bailey (Lynn) passed away on November 10, 2021, at the age of 78. She was known for her devotion to family, her service at Woolwich-Wiscasset Baptist Church, and her many summers volunteering at Living Waters with her son Stephen. She was survived by her sons James, Mark, and Stephen, her grandchildren, and extended family. Her obituary appeared in the* Wiscasset Newspaper.

End of Scene 14

Scene 15: The Mustang

MEMOIR NARRATION (DANA, to audience): *Merle, husband of Kim at the time (Angela's youngest sister), loves cars. He often tells me about various cars for sale at good deals in different places. We have these conversations, usually with little intent of taking financial action, but we love to talk about cars anyway.*

I love cars but don't know much about working on them. Beetle both loves cars and knows enough to tinker.

Merle mentions to Beetle and me that there's a 1973 Mustang Coupe for sale with a 302 engine in Connecticut for just $1,000. He continues to tell us it seems like a good deal and if Beetle and I are really thinking about working on a car together, this could be a good find.

Beetle and I think and talk about it some. It isn't too crazy of an investment, but we need to figure out how to tow it back if we get down there and like it.

So, Beetle and I put our pennies together, rent a trailer from U-Haul, and head to Connecticut to check out a potential hobby.

As you can imagine, the travel time is filled with Beetle and Dana antics. We get down there, check out the car, transact some money, and a bill of sale joins us in the cab of Beetle's truck as we venture back home with a Mustang in tow.

It's fall, and we're staying at Living Waters at the time. So, we park the car in the mostly unused carpenter shop at camp. We tinker and tinker—well, Beetle tinkers and tinkers, I just watch.

When we make purchases, we keep our receipts and don't add anything up. We just keep a mental balance of, "You bought this, so I'll buy that." With our see-saw action, we each purchase various parts.

I bought the hood, he bought a new bumper, and so on. Battery. New coil. Plugs and wires. Etc. The car turns over but doesn't start.

DANA:

I call Merle, and he says, "I'll come over and see if I can give you guys a hand."

STAGE ACTION: MERLE arrives and immediately examines things closely.

MERLE:

Hmm. It looks like the carb needs some work.

MEMOIR NARRATION (DANA): The dangerous duo's head-scratching, now joined with Merle's seemingly limitless vehicle knowledge, finally starts the car.

Merle uses a variety of tactics, saying, "Let's try this," then, "Let's try that." Finally, after some mysterious tinkering:

SOUND EFFECT: VROOM, VROOM, PUTTER, BLAHHH… Goes the engine.

BEETLE:

BLAHHH! Yup, that's what it sounded like.

STAGE ACTION: MERLE looks even more closely and does some analysis in his head.

MERLE:

Here's what I bet. I bet the guys that put this 4-barrel Holley carb on here just threw it on without coolant and tried to see if the car would fire up. It only takes a few seconds without coolant to screw up a motor.

Yeah, this has got problems. Not much compression. It probably needs to have the engine rebuilt. I know these guys that do engine work. Let me see what this will cost.

STAGE ACTION: Calling from a cell phone and going back and forth a bit, MERLE comes back with:

MERLE:

It will probably be about $850 to have it rebuilt, depending on what other issues they find.

BEETLE:

Whelp. Not much we can do but pull the engine then.

MEMOIR NARRATION (DANA): The following weekend, Merle comes back with a truck, an engine lift, and some beefier tools.

We pull out the engine in just a couple hours, and the body of the Mustang sits lifeless with its heart and soul removed and on display for any passerby to see.

About two weeks later, Merle calls us back.

MERLE:

It's done, and good news—the rest of the engine was in decent shape. They did hone out the cylinders and increased the ring size, but it's good to go and maybe has a handful more horsepower.

DANA:

Awesome!

MEMOIR NARRATION (DANA): The following weekend, Merle brings the retooled engine back to the lifeless Mustang body for the soul and body to become reunited with gas-ignited thunder and victory!

Putting the engine back in definitely takes longer than removing it, but the engine goes back in. Then, piece by piece, we add the hoses, wires for the distributor, starter wire, until every contraption is properly connected. Most importantly, we properly add the coolant.

Then it happens. History is made.

Beetle gets in. Merle adds a bit of fuel straight into the carb's bowl. Beetle turns the key, and after a little sputtering:

SOUND EFFECT: VRROOOOMMM! VROOM, VROOM, VROOM, VROOM

STAGE ACTION: As BEETLE pumps the gas. The little shop space we've borrowed billows with the smoke and life of a '73 Mustang Coupe.

MERLE:

Let's take it for a spin.

MEMOIR NARRATION (DANA): So Merle gets all his tools out of its path, and I hop in the passenger seat. Beetle takes me for a loop around camp. We go down the little hill at Butterfield Landing, and I begin to sweat as Beetle holds the brake pedal to the floor while we barely slow. There are hardly any brakes to speak of, and there's water straight ahead.

He swings us into the camp's lower driveway with more than normal G-force and says:

BEETLE:

Well… the brakes could use some work!

MEMOIR NARRATION (DANA): We continue to tinker on the car for a few more weeks, but really, it's going to take a bit more than what we've accomplished to really bring the car back into its full glory. The fun we have tops off our tanks, as tanking up on such experiences is the objective. After putting new wheels and tires on it, to pretty it up a bit, we decided to sell the car.

When we sit down to do the math, Beetle brings his receipts, and I have my pile on a table. We add up one pile. Then we add up the other pile.

STAGE ACTION: BEETLE starts laughing.

BEETLE:

How much did you say you spent?

DANA:

$1,813.25

BEETLE:

Add 'em up again.

MEMOIR NARRATION (DANA, to audience): *So, we add them again.*

BEETLE:

Now, let the record show that neither of us had added anything up, just kept rough tallies in our heads. Dana's total was $1,813.25. My total was $1,813.15. The difference between us is 10 cents.

STAGE ACTION: BEETLE reaches into his pocket, pulls out a nickel.

BEETLE:

Here ya go! Now we're even!

MEMOIR NARRATION (DANA): *It takes a couple months to sell the Mustang, which I truly regret. I wish we had kept it. In all, we ended up with about $1,600 profit to split, had some great laughs, and made some memories that will be forever cherished.*

Our lives are changing. Though we're still having fun together, our responsibilities in life are taking us in different directions. For me, I'm a dad by now and about to become one again soon. My wife and I purchased a house. I need more consistent work to raise my family. Beetle also has shifting responsibilities. Living in remote Maine, where the economy isn't really booming, leads him into all sorts of odd jobs.

We have some more fun stories to go through, but we will soon transition into the most challenging point of Beetle's life.

End of Scene 15

END OF ACT III

ACT IV
The Breaking
and the Mending.

"Anything will burn."
- Beetle

Scene 16: Danforth Shenanigans

Tableau 1 – The Hardware Store Ambush

STAGE LIGHTS: Spotlight on the darkened hardware store aisle.

STAGE ACTION: DANA crouches behind shelves. BEETLE paces like a hunter plotting.

BEETLE (whispering to Dana):

Steve Stratigos opens up at 6:50 every Saturday. Still dark. He'll never see it coming.

DANA (aside, memoir voice):

Beetle worked part-time there in the off-season. He knew every creak of that building.

SOUND EFFECT: Car pulls up, jingling keys.

BEETLE (low growl):

Grrrr!

STEVE STRATIGOS (entering, screaming):

AHHH!

DANA (jumping out, screeching):

RAHHHH!

STEVE (scrambling backward, fumbling for lights):

AHHHHH!

STAGE ACTION: BEETLE & DANA collapse in laughter, slapping knees.

DANA (to audience, memoir voice, catching breath):

Steve didn't think it was nearly as funny as we did.

Tableau 2 – Rocket Club

STAGE LIGHTS: Spotlight on a long table filled with cardboard tubes, rocket motors, switches, wires.

STAGE ACTION: BEETLE fiddles with an absurdly large rocket. DANA holds a tiny "missile."

BEETLE (to audience):

Steve wanted his rocket to look cool. Mine had to fly straight. His had fifty engines glued together.

DANA (aside, memoir voice):

It was a "Super Mega Rocket." Steve swore he had the ignition covered.

STEVE STRATIGOS (confidently):

Three… two… one… BLASTOFF!

SOUND EFFECT: Explosion of smoke. Rocket corkscrews sideways into the woods.

BEETLE (yelling, running off stage):

Forest fire! Forest fire!

STEVE (stomping):

There's smoke over here!

STAGE ACTION: BEETLE & DANA laughing hysterically as they help stomp.

DANA (to audience, memoir voice):

He still laughs about it every time he tells it.

Closing Reflection

DANA (stepping forward, memoir voice, softer)

We were in our thirties and forties then. Still pulling the same stunts, still laughing until our sides ached. The mischief never really left us — it just found new hiding places.

STAGE LIGHTS: Lights dim.

End of Scene 16

Scene 17: Doing So Much for So Many

Opening

DANA (to audience, memoir voice):

Beetle gave his time everywhere — farm, school, church, store, even the wastewater plant. You couldn't walk down Main Street without hearing, "Hey Beetle!" So instead of telling you, let me show you.

Cameo 1 – Apgar Farm

(A *cameo* is a brief appearance by a character who is not central to the scene but adds color, humor, or recognition. In this script, cameos allow friends, family, or community members to step in briefly with a memorable line or presence.)

STAGE LIGHTS: Spotlight on BEETLE as he enters holding a turkey under each arm. Dave Apgar walks onto the stage in his overalls and barn jacket.

DAVE APGAR:

Beetle, we have turkeys coming in on Thursday and I need...

BEETLE (interrupting):

I know, I know. You want me to feed, water, and babysit a bunch of the dumbest creatures on the planet.

BEETLE (to the audience, rolling his eyes):

Turkeys! Dumbest birds alive. Don't move their water or they'll die of thirst.

DANA (aside, memoir voice):

Still, he kept them alive. They thought he was their mama.

BEETLE (repulsed):

I ain't their mama!

Cameo 2 – Dave's Hardware Store

STAGE LIGHTS: Spotlight on BEETLE in an apron, putting a hammer into a small display of items on sale.

CUSTOMER (offstage):

Beetle, you got a minute?

BEETLE (checking his wristwatch and walking toward the voice):

Whelp, let me see. Yup, I got a minute. You got one, too?

STAGE ACTION: BEETLE assists the customer.

DANA (aside):

He was tried and true with his work at the hardware store. Anytime the owners needed anything, he was there.

BEETLE (finishing up with the customer):

That'll be a THOUSAND DOLLARS!

CUSTOMER:

Yeah, I've heard that before!

BEETLE (confirming with his watch):

Oh, and you said it was only gonna take a minute. Looks like it took two.

Cameo 3 – Wreath Factory

STAGE LIGHTS: Spotlight on BEETLE in a Santa hat, arms full of wreaths. TASHA, a worker, appears on the stage working at a table.

BEETLE (grinning):

December 1st? Hat's on. No exceptions.

TASHA:

Hey Beetle, I've got a load of centerpieces over here.

Beetle bends down to pick up a box on one knee.

TASHA (continuing):

Oh Beetle, I thought you'd never ask!

BEETLE (turning to the audience):

Ever been engaged to a married woman!?

DANA (aside, pointing to the hat):

Oh, and that Santa hat... he wore that thing everywhere — even to church.

Cameo 4 – Bus Driver

STAGE LIGHTS: Spotlight on BEETLE at a steering wheel, Santa hat still on, honks horn.

BEETLE (calling out):

Seat belts, kids. Even pranksters need to ride safe.

DANA (aside):

From prankster to protector — he took it seriously.

STAGE ACTION: Kids getting on the bus.

BEETLE (dead serious to Dana):

Prankster!? Where'd you get that idea!?

Cameo 5 – Janitor

STAGE LIGHTS: Spotlight on BEETLE as he mops the floor.

BEETLE (matter-of-factly):

Process is the key. Stick to the process and do it right.

DANA (aside):

Even sweeping floors, he did it with vigilance.

BEETLE:

GUM! I hate gum.

Cameo 6 – Food Pantry

STAGE LIGHTS: Spotlight on. MARILYN STODDARD enters, clipboard in hand.

MARILYN:

Beetle, we need help with the truck.

BEETLE (pretending to sigh):

Today?! I was gonna give my dog, Max, a bath.

MARILYN:

Can you give him a bath tomorrow?

BEETLE (with a smirk):

I dunno, it seems like he should get a bath at least once a year and this is that day. Oh wait a sec, it was me that needed a bath and I took one last night. Yeah, I guess I can help then.

DANA (aside):

He always showed up. Always.

MARILYN:

Yes he did!

Cameo 7 – Wastewater Plant

STAGE LIGHTS: Spotlight on BEETLE with a rubber ball with lights on it.

DMITRIY:

Beetle, I'm glad you are at least wearing gloves. But that thing is cool. It looks like one of those kids toys that bounces all around and lights up.

BEETLE (laughing to DMITRIY):

Yeah, can you believe this came through the sewer! Who in town pooped *this* out?

SOUND EFFECT: Audience groans and laughs.

Closing Reflection

DANA (to audience):

From farms to schools, from wreaths to wastewater — Beetle worked everywhere, gave everywhere. Not for money, but because people needed him. That's who he was.

STAGE LIGHTS: Lights dim.

End of Scene 17

Scene 18: Whiteman Backstory

MEMOIR NARRATION (DANA): *It is critical to set some backstory about the Whitemans.*

Around 2001 to 2003 (the exact year is fuzzy), I had the opportunity to meet Stan and Mary Ellen Whiteman. I was helping perform some site surveys for an internet provider. Until that point, Danforth was solely equipped with dial-up internet.

Let's be honest—there isn't much good to be said about dial-up internet. It allows you to get your email and do some very basic browsing. It also allows you to get a cup of coffee, make a full meal, and consume it before a single modern webpage opens.

My Job as a Site Surveyor Works Like This

MEMOIR NARRATION (DANA): *Someone called me and made an appointment to have their location checked for internet availability. I drove out to the site and checked it with portable equipment. If their location could receive internet, they signed an installation form, and I let the internet service provider know. They then scheduled an installation.*

This "over the air" internet used 900MHz radios and was very slow but much faster than dial-up. Those who were desperate to see the online world through more than a small opening scraped into the ice of the internet windshield after a storm were thrilled to get a full panorama of websites, online video, and limitless email.

I knocked on the door of the Whitemans and met Stan along with two small barking pomeranians.

SOUND EFFECT: Sound of knocking and dogs barking.

MEMOIR NARRATION (DANA): *Maggie (brown and the noisiest) and Bear (grey, who just wanted to lick me after I put my hand down). Stan introduced himself—a tall, thin man with grey hair, somewhere near the age of eighty. Immediately, Stan offered me coffee from the swankiest coffee machine in Danforth, perhaps the county.*

Stan and I chatted for a bit while the expensive Jura coffee machine chopped up my beans and made me an excellent cup of coffee. All the while, I was thinking, "Why does this old man need the internet?" Boy, did I have a lot to learn.

STAGE ACTION: STAN walks DANA in the living room where MARY ELLEN sat in a chair, reading a book.

STAN (gesturing to Dana):

This is Dana. He is here to see about the faster internet.

MARY ELLEN (looking over her glasses):

Hello.

MEMOIR NARRATION (DANA): Mary Ellen seemed to be in her late sixties or early seventies. Charlie, a parrot, was in a cage in the corner making some whistles and other noises.

At that point, I realized there was a need for faster internet. Behind the couch where Mary Ellen sat, there is a Power Mac G4 with an enormous screen. Knowing my computers well, I recognized that this was an expensive computer that was likely crippled by slow internet.

These were interesting people with very interesting tastes.

You know when you meet someone interesting and never want to forget it? That's what happened to me that day.

STAN:

Let's go upstairs.

MEMOIR NARRATION (DANA): He led me from Kansas into the world of Oz, from black and white into the full color spectrum of all things electronic. Stan's persona received an instant upgrade in my mind—from everyday old folk to hero.

He had radios, computer parts kicking around, electronic kits of various sorts, and projects everywhere. Not to mention beautiful paintings. He was an exceptionally gifted man, and my intrigue about him, his history, his wife's history, and all things Whiteman was piqued.

Stan sat me down at his modern computer, running over a 3GHz Pentium 4 CPU. I realize that might not mean much to you, but it was fast for its day—a very snappy modern machine that wasn't cheap.

The Whiteman's got their internet upgrade. Their location provided some challenges due to a hill near their house, but I made sure something could be figured out to improve their online experiences.

Over the years, my love for the Whitemans outgrew its initial infatuation with electronics and stories—stories I won't get into here. This is a book about Beetle, not the Whitemans (though that could also fill multiple volumes on its own). Stan and I grew close, and I considered him my adopted grandfather and Mary Ellen, eventually, as my adopted grandmother.

I was never close to either set of my grandparents—something I regret—but distance and life situations kept me from knowing them well. Here, however, was an older couple that I could get to know. I cherished any time I got to spend with them.

Many back-to-back Saturdays, Stan and I worked on various projects: antennas, computer problems, scanning photos into the computer (photography was another of his passions), and whatever the "issue of the day" provided for problems.

MARY ELLEN:

Stan! You have too many hobbies!

MEMOIR NARRATION (DANA): As Stan grew in age, we both grew up. Stan and Mary Ellen educated me on many travels around the globe. Saturday after Saturday, I sat and drank coffee for hours, usually beginning by 9 AM and ending around 11 AM, and sometimes even later.

This becomes a ritual. In fact, if I didn't show up around nine, I would receive a call: "Dana, you coming over today? … Good, I have a story I forgot to tell you about."

In 2007, Aaron was born. Angela and I took our newborn and Caleb over to meet Stan and Mary Ellen. Mary Ellen smiled from ear to ear. They never had children, and they both fell in love with ours.

Sometime after that, Sunday afternoons with Stan and Mary Ellen were firmly established, with Beetle eventually joining in as well. Angela or Beetle often made lunch, or we might order out from the Mill Yard. Caleb had a servant's heart and gladly made us sodas using a soda-making gadget that Mary Ellen couldn't resist purchasing specifically for our Sunday occasions together.

Week after week, this is what we did. Stan, Mary Ellen, Caleb, Aaron, Angela, Beetle, and I were bonded into a deep relationship with each other. Stan and Mary Ellen were an older couple who had nothing but smiles and warm hospitality to offer us, along with their years of gleaning wisdom from life.

In classic Beetle fashion, Beetle told various stories and escapades of he and I growing up and all the life experiences God had given us over the years.

Around 2012, Stan suffered a life-altering stroke. Stan could no longer speak. While he could make parts of words, the syllables were all jumbled. He thought he knew what he was saying, from the expression on his face, but we just couldn't understand him. However, he seemed to understand everything we were saying and smiled and laughed along with us.

Stan was determined, though. Being verbally crippled didn't handicap his warm smile. He instead used his facial expressions and hand motions to send us codes about what he needed and when he needed it.

End of Scene 18

Scene 19: Beetle the Caretaker

STAGE LIGHTS: Soft, warm glow.

STAGE ACTION: A hospital bed downstage left. STAN lies in bed, frail. MARY ELLEN sits close by.

DANA (seated at bedside, Bible open, reading slowly):

"In the beginning was the Word, and the Word was with God, and the Word was God."

BEETLE (standing near head of bed, gently adjusting pillows, steadying STAN as he shifts):

Easy now, Stan… we've got you.

MARY ELLEN (quietly, with gratitude):

Thank you, Beetle.

STAGE ACTION: STAN smiles faintly, eyes closed.

DANA (continues reading, softer):

"The light shines in the darkness, and the darkness has not overcome it."

STAGE ACTION: TABLEAU FREEZES: DANA and reading at bedside, BEETLE standing watch, MARY ELLEN'S close by.

MEMOIR NARRATION: DANA (steps forward, memoir voice): I had sat with Stan many Saturdays, listening to his stories. But when words left him after the stroke, Beetle and I became his words — through presence, through prayer, through care.

Beetle, who never thought of himself as a caretaker, showed up every time. He lifted when strength was needed, he listened when silence was all Stan could give, and he became the steady anchor Mary Ellen leaned on.

In those moments, Beetle's humor faded into gentleness. His consistency, his faithfulness — that was his gift to Stan. It was a different kind of laughter, one rooted in hope, that carried us all through those final days.

STAGE LIGHTS: Lights fade to black.

End of Scene 19

Scene 20: Apart

STAGE LIGHTS: Heavenly glow.

GOD:

Have you considered my servant Beetle? Even in caretaking, he gave his all for Stan.

SATAN (hissing in disgust):

AHH! When you let me take Beetle and Dana apart, you limited my time. Should they be apart longer, Beetle will lose all joy.

GOD:

Okay, move Dana. Nothing more.

STAGE LIGHTS: Spotlight returns to earth.

STAGE ACTION (projected or narrated): "July 2014 – Dana moves to Raleigh, North Carolina."

MEMOIR NARRATION (DANA): *In July of 2014, I abruptly left my work at the Hodgdon School Department when I accepted a role in Raleigh, North Carolina. I'm sure it was a shock to Beetle, but God had provided in ways that Angela and I could not ignore, and we knew we needed to take this leap of faith. We enrolled Aaron, now seven, and Caleb, now fourteen, into GRACE Christian School, where I became a computer science and multimedia teacher for both middle school and high school grades.*

The transition to North Carolina left no room for warning. When I officially received the position, I was to report for work in just four days. I accepted the role on a Wednesday, gave notice on a Thursday, packed up on Friday, began the drive on Saturday, showed up for a school meet-and-greet event on Sunday, and started work on Monday.

It was chaos.

BEETLE (with a sigh):

Yeah, those weren't good times.

STAGE ACTION (projected or narrated mid-scene): "2014–2015 – Long-distance calls with Beetle continue weekly."

MEMOIR NARRATION (DANA): *Additionally, though we were in North Carolina, Beetle still goes to Mary Ellen's each Sunday, where we would catch up with each other in the form of a video call. We caught up on the news of the week, prayed together, and read Scripture together.*

The Moose Hunt

MEMOIR NARRATION (DANA): *Beetle was a lucky duck. I remember one time at random when he fired his slingshot across a stream, just having fun. At complete random, he downed a small bird that flew into the rock's path. He saw it go down and really felt bad about it. He didn't fire the slingshot much more that day.*

But this was the kind of luck we needed. We had been itching to go on a moose hunt, and the chances were slim. In the black hole where the Maine Fisheries and Wildlife sticks the money from people's lottery entries into the Moose Hunt system, never to be seen again, somehow Beetle's name got drawn!

STAGE ACTION (projected or narrated): "Summer 2015 – Beetle's name is drawn in the Maine Moose Permit Lottery."

BEETLE:

I'll give you three guesses what just happened?

DANA:

What?

BEETLE:

You have to guess!

DANA:

You got a brand new truck?

BEETLE:

Nope.

DANA:

Max got his driver's license?

MEMOIR NARRATION (DANA, to audience): *Max is his dog.*

BEETLE:

Nope.

DANA:

You made supper?

BEETLE:

Well, yeah, of course I made supper, but that's not it! Dave was checking online and called me just now to tell me that I got my Moose permit!

MEMOIR NARRATION (DANA): *Yes, this is the same Dave that was our youth leader growing up. He also moved to the Danforth area and was a Registered Maine Guide, keeping his eye on the State of Maine Moose Permit Lottery.*

DANA:

Awesome!

BEETLE:

Well, I have a problem. I'm trying to figure out who I can put down as my number two.

DANA:

Uhhh...

BEETLE (laughing):

Just kidding! Of course I put you down!

MEMOIR NARRATION (DANA): I had a commitment to keep, even if we had moved to North Carolina between the time of Beetle getting his moose permit and the actual hunt.

DANA:

Saweeet!

MEMOIR NARRATION (DANA): Now, there was a problem. Neither Beetle nor I had ever been moose hunting. In fact, neither of us had even shot a deer. We didn't know where to go hunting in the zone he had selected or even how to dress out a moose.

So, we talked to Dave.

We knocked on Dave's door.

DAVE:

Come in. Well, looky what we have here—you two pranksters actually have to come to me for some hunting advice. Isn't this a switch?

He laughs.

MEMOIR NARRATION (DANA): Beetle and I probably just looked dumb and goofy to him. He was the master of the moose, the Wildman of the wood, the connoisseur of the canoe, and we were helplessly looking for advice.

Dave puts his hands to his mouth and makes some call that sounds like a young calf.

DAVE:

MWWaaaahhhhh.

MEMOIR NARRATION (DANA, to audience): *He calls out with a throaty, yet somehow nasally, sound. He does it again. We are just laughing at the sound.*

DAVE:

For real, that's the call you need to make. You try it?

MEMOIR NARRATION (DANA): *At this point, I was personally convinced that he was screwing around with us to get a good laugh at his kitchen table and probably had some hidden game camera set up to capture us looking like morons so he could post it on YouTube. Nope. Not me.*

Beetle didn't take the bait either.

DAVE:

Look guys, for real, this is what you do.

MEMOIR NARRATION (DANA, to audience): *He calls out again.*

DAVE:

MWAAaahhh!

MEMOIR NARRATION (DANA): *Well, I guessed if Dave was doing this, then that same footage of us acting like idiots would also capture Dave himself acting like an idiot, so I gave it a try.*

DANA:

MWWaaahhhh.

DAVE:

No, make the aaahh longer.

DANA:

MWWAAAAhhhhh.

DAVE:

You got it, that's it! You need to keep practicing that. You need to get comfortable with it.

MEMOIR NARRATION (DANA): *At this point, I was ready to hear Dave give some sage advice like, "Be one with the moose and he will be one with you," but that advice never came.*

STAGE ACTION: Next, DAVE picks up a broom.

DAVE:

This is key now. As soon as you know that you are being spotted by the moose, Dana, your job is to help Beetle get the shot, so you need to take your rifle, hold it over your head with both hands like this...

STAGE ACTION: DAVE taking the broom and holding it just over his head.

DAVE:

...and wobble back and forth like this.

MEMOIR NARRATION (DANA, to audience): *He looks like a drunk moose in his living room.*

STAGE ACTION: BEETLE and DANA just laugh and laugh.

DAVE:

For real, the moose can't see well. He sees Dana as if he is another bull moose and wants to challenge it. At this point, things can get dicey. You don't want to call him so close that he charges you. Dana, people have died that way. But when he starts in your direction, Beetle, you need to square up your shot, exhale, and squeeze that trigger.

MEMOIR NARRATION (DANA): *We practiced looking like idiots for a while, taking turns making the moose call and looking like a drunken moose.*

DAVE:

Now, dressing out a moose is like dressing out a deer. Just bigger.

DANA:

Uh, but Dave, neither of us has dressed out a deer.

MEMOIR NARRATION (DANA): *Audience discretion is advised.*

So, Dave explained in detail exactly what to do. I'll spare you the explanation.

At some point in dressing out a moose, one needs to take their entire arm and put it up into the neck to cut the wind pipe. Actually, it takes two hands. So, you can look forward to either me or Beetle with both hands at least up to our elbows inside a moose's neck. I apologize if I'm grossing you out right now, but it gets comedic later.

Dave also took out a map and showed us some good areas to hunt in the zone for which Beetle had selected.

In truth, we never saw nor heard anything of hidden footage of our pre-moose-hunting practice in Dave's kitchen, so I'm pretty sure by now we were in the clear.

Hunting Week

MEMOIR NARRATION (DANA, to audience): *I hurried back from North Carolina to go moose hunting with Beetle. Since it is soon after we moved, I need to prepare a moving truck to get some remaining things out of the house and move them into storage. It was going to be a busy week, but the moose hunt takes priority over everything else. I arrived on Saturday in Maine. Beetle* *and I packed up our things on a Sunday and even had access to a four-wheeler in case we needed some engine power to pull a moose out of the woods.*

With everything packed and ready to go, we hit the road. We undoubtedly sang "Cash Cow" by Steve Taylor and played some of our other old favorites.

STAGE ACTION (projected or narrated mid-scene): "October 2015 – Moose Hunt, Northern Maine."

MEMOIR NARRATION (DANA): *We camped outside for the night on a Sunday evening on a cold October day. It was 30-something degrees when we got up, and we really didn't sleep that well. After getting some breakfast, we got a late start to the woods.*

We finally made it to a nice clearing we had scoped out the day before.

Hunting anything can be a long process with little results. But it went kinda like this.

BEETLE:

You hear that?

DANA:

Yeah, sounds like something in the woods.

BEETLE:

Yeah, why don't you do that moose call thing.

STAGE ACTION: Dana attempts the moose call.

DANA:

MWWAAAAaaahhhh. MWWAAAAaaaahhhh.

MEMOIR NARRATION (DANA): *The sound is made by holding your hands over your mouth and nose, as if you were going to sneeze, then gradually opening them up with a nasally sort of call while making a "mmaaaahhh" sound.*

Monday came and went. Nothing.

Fortunately for us, we no longer had to sleep in a tent as the owner of the campground had a cabin open up when a couple of other moose hunters were victorious on day one of their hunt.

Ahh… nice warm quarters for the night.

Tuesday arrives.

MEMOIR NARRATION (DANA): *We saw some tracks, fresh and good sized, and heard some pretty big moose thrashing around in the woods, but we didn't see it. We stayed until dusk, and then we saw a cow moose. "Perfect. We'll come right back here tomorrow and see if a bull shows up."*

Wednesday morning arrives.

MEMOIR NARRATION (DANA): *Beetle and I got out early, a little after six. Rather than lollygagging with breakfast, we each took a few breakfast bars and had a lunch ready to go that was prepared from the night before.*

We arrived for day three, parked the truck, and walked slowly into view of the field where we had seen the cow. Nothing. It was super quiet this particular morning.

BEETLE:

Hey, do your thing.

MEMOIR NARRATION (DANA, to audience): *I repeat the moose call, waiting a few seconds between each call.*

DANA:

MWWAAaaahhh! … MWWWAAAaaahhhh!

BEETLE (excitedly):

Oh, oh, did you hear that!

MEMOIR NARRATION (DANA): *To our left was the field where we saw the cow, but straight ahead was a skidder trail leading up a hill into the woods. There was some serious thrashing around out there.*

Everything goes still again.

I call out again.

DANA:

MWWAAahhhh!

MEMOIR NARRATION (DANA): *Oh, if Dave could see me now, I must be a pro at this.*

SOUND EFFECTS: CRASH! THUMP!

BEETLE (excitedly):

Straight ahead, there he is!

MEMOIR NARRATION (DANA): *There is a bull moose, not sure how many points, but there he is, standing on the skidder trail, looking around with curiosity.*

DANA:

Beetle, you get up there near the edge of the trees and let me see if I can draw him out where you can get a shot.

MEMOIR NARRATION (DANA, to audience): *The moose saunters down the hill right into Beetle's sights and BAM! The moose dropped like a rock.*

Beetle and I hoop and holler and give each other high five's.

MEMOIR NARRATION (DANA, to audience): *I had even started to think like Dave, and that was scary.*

Gleefully, Beetle and I headed out to see his victory when, uh, we began sinking. This would-be trail was actually a muck-filled gully. We were up to our ankles. Then up to our calves. Then up to our knees. Finally, up to our mid-thighs.

Wading in the mud, we finally reach the moose.

DANA:

Six points.

BEETLE:

Not huge, but will have some good meat. Should be nice and tender.

DANA:

How on earth are we going to get this thing out of here?

BEETLE:

Whelp, we have the four-wheeler. Let's get the truck and get the four-wheeler off and see what we have to work with.

MEMOIR NARRATION (DANA): *After backing the four-wheeler up to the edge of the muck, we realized that we didn't have nearly enough rope. Beetle dug around behind the seats and found more pieces of rope here and there.*

We tied all the rope together to make up the nearly 150 feet that was needed to pull this creature out of its natural habitat and into our stomachs. We hadn't even dressed it out yet. We really didn't want mud-filled moose stew, even though that's exactly what I was standing in.

The rope was barely long enough. In hindsight, maybe we should have called the moose just a little closer before taking the shot, but there are no mulligans in hunting.

We hooked up the four-wheeler, and Beetle took up the slack, then started to throttle a little.

SOUND EFFECT: SNAP!

DANA:

There's some weak rope that's got to go.

BEETLE:

Hmm… the tie-down straps are strong. Let's get that old rope out and put some straps in.

MEMOIR NARRATION (DANA): So that's what we did.

Beetle needed to pull the moose straight, but there wasn't that much gravel road to use, and the moose only moved a few feet at a time. It was like watching a rubber band being used to pull an object across the surface of a desk. You pull a lot, the rubber band stretches out, then the object moves just a little.

The moose moved a few feet. Then we reseted the four-wheeler, took up some slack, and tried again. The moose moves a few more feet. Repeat. Repeat. Each time we took up about 10 feet of the nearly 150-foot line.

At 2:00 PM, after seven hours of wrestling with the moose, it was finally time to dress it out.

We took turns with the various maneuvers Dave so eloquently taught us, and we actually received some good compliments on it later. But then, we had to determine who was going to cut the windpipe.

It was me.

Again, audience discretion is advised.

MEMOIR NARRATION (DANA, to audience): It was unforgetta-ble. We had everything complete except the last crucial step—cutting the wind-pipe. So, I laid on the ground and decided I will need some sort of device, like used in the movie "Men in Black", to erase my memory once this job was completed. I had hoped Beetle brought one with him. I laid on my side and I slid both my arms up in unison, elbow deep now into a real moose. I must have looked like I was getting ready to put it on like a costume. Slice. The job was done.

DANA:

I think I'll be ready for a shower when we get outta here.

MEMOIR NARRATION (DANA): *We finished dressing it out in a record 90 minutes. It was a personal best, but yeah, we were slow.*

It was now 3:30 PM.

Loading the moose onto the trailer wasn't nearly as eventful as getting him out of the mud. We took off.

At 4:00 PM, we were finally eating our lunch after an exhausting moose expedition. To any passerby that might have observed us, they would have said, "They must not be from around here."

We got back to our cabin, loaded up our gear, and headed to a game weigh station. We called around, and some game stations had closed early, so we had to go out of our way by about 30 minutes to one that would be open by the time we reached it.

As we pulled in, someone said:

GAME WARDEN:

Hey, good job dressing out that moose!

BEETLE & DANA (in unison):

Hey, thanks.

MEMOIR NARRATION (DANA): *At the Game Warden's comments Beetle and I just looked at each other and kept the laughter bottled up as we were the only ones that knew it took us well over an hour to dress out that moose.*

But through the smiles, neither of us wanted anything more than to get home, shower, and sleep.

If I remember right, it weighed in at 490 pounds dressed. Not a huge moose, but man, that's a lot of weight.

End of Scene 20

Scene 21: Treasure Hunting

BEETLE (to audience):

Three guesses what's next.

DANA:

I'll throw it out there.

BEETLE:

Oh, I don't need any guesses. Next to camp, this is pretty much my favorite thing. TREASURE HUNTING!

Captain Kidd's Treasure

MEMOIR NARRATION (DANA): Even though I was living in North Carolina, every summer Beetle and I planned what we were going to do for fun when the time allowed us to be back together. We took advantage of as much time together, as little as it was.

DANA:

Hey Beet, what kind of mischief are we going to get into this summer? It's just a couple weeks away!

BEETLE:

Well… I tell ya what… I heard that Captain Kidd had a treasure kept somewhere in the area.

DANA:

Where?

BEETLE:

I'm not sure, but it might have been right in Wiscasset.

DANA:

So where do we go looking?

BEETLE:

We can go right in back of my parents' house down to the water. I mean, if he did bury a treasure, why not there?

MEMOIR NARRATION (DANA): Beetle's logic was interesting. He had a "why not?" way of thinking.

DANA:

Sounds good.

BEETLE:

I've got Stan's old metal detector. Mary Ellen told me to keep it after Stan passed. So we'll just grab some shovels and go for it.

DANA:

Wicked good!

MEMOIR NARRATION (DANA): That's what we did. We went to Beetle's parents' house, walked down to the water, and began detecting metal objects with the hopes that we'd get a metal detection off the charts and a chest full of gold.

SOUND EFFECT: WIZZZ, WIZZZ was the sound the detector made.

BEETLE:

Oh, oh, oh, here's something.

MEMOIR NARRATION (DANA): With a small garden spade, I got down and dug up a clump of dirt. Beetle then scanned the hole, then the dirt to make sure that whatever the object was, we had pulled it into the pile.

Another WIZZZ confirms it.

BEETLE

Yup, you got it.

MEMOIR NARRATION (DANA): *Spreading it out, I held up our first find.*

DANA:

Beetle, it's a spent .22 cartridge.

BEETLE:

Keep it.

MEMOIR NARRATION (DANA): *Beetle kept everything from our escapades.*

SOUND EFFECT: WIZZZ, WIZZZ came from the detector again.

MEMOIR NARRATION (DANA): *Another .22 cartridge. Then another. Then a spent shotgun shell. Then more .22 casings. Then there was something different—a bottle cap.*

The .22 casings are the closest we got to gold that day, as they were gold-colored brass. Well, it was brass that turned green and was corroded by the weather, but in our minds, it glistened like gold.

I must point out that Captain Kidd having any sort of treasure in or near Wiscasset, Maine, was complete conjecture. Many historians doubt that Kidd ever made it to the Maine coast. But facts don't always make the best documentaries, and if rumors of a treasure had never hit Beetle's ears, then he and I might have had some great memories stolen from us. So, to that we say, thank you for the rumor! It was great fun!

DANA:

Hmm… Beetle, we need to find a better treasure location. We burned through that summer's fun, so the next treasure hunt will have to wait a full year.

Magnet Fishing

MEMOIR NARRATION (DANA): Beetle and I also tried our hand at magnet fishing. It works like this: Bait a rope with a magnet and put it in the water. If a piece of metal thinks it can take on that magnet, it will bite. Pull it up and see what kind of metal fish you get.

As a birthday present to Beetle and myself (since we share the same birthday), I purchased two magnet fishing kits online and then headed north to Maine that summer to see what Beetle and I could find.

We found some cool things. We would go to various bridges in the area and don't really find much. But then, in Danforth, we pulled up axe head after axe head, wondering if an axe delivery truck must have gone off the bridge.

Bub Bailey Gold Prospect

DANA:

How about we find a location that actually was known to have gold? I remember Stan talking about gold being not too far from Danforth.

BEETLE:

Got any idea how we find that spot?

DANA:

Not really. Let's do some research.

MEMOIR NARRATION (DANA): I do indeed remember Stan talking about gold in Danforth. He said it was near Greenland Cove, but I can't remember the exact details. If Beetle had been with me when Stan mentioned it, then I'm sure he would have remembered.

So, we got on a computer and started researching.

There are references to gold, but nothing concrete. But then, jackpot! Or actually what we hoped for was a pre-jackpot, with the real jackpot being that we would find the location and gold would pour itself into our pockets, straight from the ground.

Online, we found a document titled, "Bedrock Geology of the Grand Lake Area, Aroostook, Hancock, Penobscot, and Washington Counties, Maine." It was a scanned document that references the following:

"The abandoned Bub Bailey gold prospect, northwest of Flagstaff Mountain, in the Danforth quadrangle (pl. 1), was reported by Mr. G. F. Kinney, of Danforth, was opened about 1890. It was worked by Bub Bailey in the period 1920-25, and last worked for a short time in 1953 by John Kelly, of Bangor, assisted by Mr. Kinney."

"The prospect is on land now reportedly owned by the St. Regis Paper Co. The prospect is a small trench that follows a quartz vein trending N. 24° W. and dipping 85° NE. Slickensides rake 25° SE. The vein is reported to have ranged from 2 to 6 inches in width; it cuts contact-metamorphosed gray sericitic metasiltstone and impure quartzite containing biotite and retrograded cordierite. The cut, excavated by hand methods, ranges from 4 to 6 feet in depth, 2 to 5 feet in width, and is about 50 feet long. Only a trace, if any, of gold was found by the prospectors, and the material remaining in the dump is apparently unmineralized."

That's it. I didn't know what half of it meant. What on earth is a slickenside? We showed the document to my dad, a matter-of-fact real-life gold panner and dredger and the only one I knew that had the key to decrypt this jumble of code.

The coolest thing of all, though, was that the man that discovered the site is a Bailey! Now another Bailey circles back to the site and perhaps was the last Bailey to explore it!

My dad gave us some instruction as well as access to his gold detector.

Beetle and I planned for another great time that summer together!

Now equipped with two metal detectors, one of which is calibrated to detect gold, we headed into the hills of the Flagstaff mountain area.

It might be said that if you're going to go into the woods to search for gold, you might want to know exactly where you're going. Beetle and I, armed with Beetle's "why not?" attitude, like "why not find it here" or "why not find it there," walked in circles, not having the foggiest notion where to go.

BEETLE:

Steve Gray says, "You can't miss it; you can almost see it from the road. There's a pile of rocks and a ditch."

MEMOIR NARRATION (DANA): *The instructions came from someone that had forested the woods and driven over the area with a skidder.*

"You can't miss it," echoed in our minds, meanwhile, we missed it.

We walked in circle after circle one morning. We ate lunch. Then Beetle had to work that afternoon at the hardware store, so we came back the next day.

We walked in circles some more, then ate lunch, walked a bit more, then gave up for day two.

Day three looks bleak.

DANA:

We can't just keep walking in circles.

BEETLE:

No, but I've been trying to call Steve, and there's no answer.

MEMOIR NARRATION (DANA): *This was Steven Gray, different from the other Steve mentioned.*

Beetle had to work that morning, which turned out to be to our advantage.

BEETLE:

Guess who stopped in the hardware store today? Steve!

DANA:

Awesome, did you get some more clues?

BEETLE:

He's gonna drive out there with us and show us exactly where it is!

MEMOIR NARRATION (DANA): Later on day three, our bleakness turned to joy as at last, the location where we should have been looking was cleared up! Steve showed us exactly where the mine was located.

It was already getting late on day three, so we just locked it into our memories, and its treasures would have to wait until morning.

The following morning, Beetle and I excitedly made our way out to the real Bub Bailey Gold Prospect. We stopped at the Mill Yard and had some sandwiches made in anticipation that our day would be filled with pocketing both memories and gold!

We got to the site, pulled out our detectors, and began scoping it out.

SOUND EFFECT: WIZZZ, WIZZZ went Stan's old detector that Beetle used.

It wasn't but a few seconds, and we were already getting hits. Beetle dug around a bit.

BEETLE:

Hey Dana, check this out. Looks like an old coffee pot.

DANA:

Awesome! I bet Bub Bailey used that pot himself while camping out here.

SOUND EFFECT: WIZZZ, WIZZZ went mine this time.

MEMOIR NARRATION (DANA): Beetle and I dug together and pulled up an axe head.

BEETLE:

Awesome! I bet Bub used this axe head to get wood for his fire.

SOUND EFFECT: WIZZZ, WIZZZ, WIZZZ, WIZZZ

MEMOIR NARRATION (DANA, to audience): This one was big and long!

MEMOIR NARRATION (DANA): Beetle and I grabbed what seemed like a tree root out of the ground.

BEETLE:

Holy smokes! It's a big pry bar.

DANA:

Yeah, I bet he didn't want to have to tote this big heavy thing back and forth.

MEMOIR NARRATION (DANA): But gold? Nope. We didn't find any, but we did find lots of cool stuff that day. It's probably the best treasure hunting day we ever had.

My dad was also curious about the site. He came out with Beetle and me later that summer, and we pulled and rolled every rock out of the trench and dug it down to the ledge. Dad pulled some of the gravel out and even panned out some of it. Nothing.

The conclusion from my dad was clear. Whatever gold was there, Bub Bailey had gotten it. Only rumors of the mine kept the curiosity of gold-finding wannabes coming back for more, but there was no more. Well, no more than the memories that Beetle and I established that day. Truly, those memories are worth more than any gold could ever produce.

DANA (to audience):

Now, we will pivot to ACT V – The Final Days.

BEETLE (in refusal):

Oh no you don't!

DANA:

Don't what?

BEETLE:

Skip some really great stories.

DANA:

What you got in mind?

BEETLE:

You get all these opportunities to speak to the audience in narration and junk, it's my turn! We need the house lights up!

STAGE ACTION: BACKSTAGE: Stagehands mumble as they stumble around caught off guard. Someone slowly brings up the lights in the theater.

STAGE ACTION: BEETLE scans the audience.

BEETLE:

EMMETT MAILMAN! Get up here! … and let's see… ROGER DUTTWEILER! That'll do it. Ok, you can put the lights back down.

STAGE ACTION: Hesitantly, two members of the audience come on the stage.

STAGE LIGHTS: The theater lights go back to their dimmed position and a small group of people are lit on the stage, Beetle, Dana, Emmett, and Roger.

Pig Rider

DANA (teasing):

Oh, I know where this is going!

BEETLE (positioning Emmett):

You got it! Let's see… Emmett, you gotta stand right about here. Roger… you can just stand off to the side for now.

STAGE ACTION: Roger Duttweiler shrugs his shoulders and steps backwards. BEETLE puts EMMETT in a very specific position on the stage, a rope curiously lying on the stage between his legs.

STAGE ACTION: The guests invited to the stage chuckle. Dana shakes his head.

BEETLE (wheezing laugh):

We were at camp, we were moving the pigs, which didn't want to be moved. They were in a trailer when…

STAGE ACTION: A rope makes a whizzing sound as it is dragged quickly across the stage to reveal the prop of a stuffed pig which catches EMMETT between the legs taking him backward for a ride.

EMMETT (eyes wide, riding a stuffed pig):

WHOOOAAA!!!

BEETLE (bend over, laughing hysterically, slapping his knee):

It was just like that!

STAGE ACTION: EMMETT, arms trying to find balance, flops to one side of the pig onto a pre-positioned gymnastics mat.

STAGE ACTION: AUDIENCE explodes in laughter, as do DANA and EMMETT, laughing equally with Beetle, doubled over in hysterics.

BEETLE (with a long sigh of satisfaction):

That pig caught Emmett between the legs and gave him the ride of his life! Arms-a-flailin' everywhere. "Pig Rider" was born that day.

STAGE ACTION: EMMETT rises up in laughter and holds his hands up in victory over his head.

STAGE ACTION: EMMETT starts walking away.

BEETLE:

Hang on, Emmett! I got you something.

STAGE ACTION: A stagehand throws something to BEETLE who throws it to EMMETT.

BEETLE (insistent):

Hold it up so everyone can see.

EMMETT (holding up a t-shirt):

It says, 'EMMETT MAILMAN – PIG RIDER – WORLD CHAMPION'

STAGE ACTION: EMMETT holds it proudly for everyone to see.

STAGE ACTION: The AUDIENCE stands for a moment in applause and laughter.

STAGE ACTION: EMMETT walks off stage holding the shirt high.

DANA (to audience):

And with Roger Duttweiler up here... I think I know where this is going next... One stunt, one spark, and suddenly Beetle had a story that haunted us for decades. In town, you didn't just hear about Beetle. You heard about... WOOF JUICE! For a long time, the two were synonymous and to some people they still are!

BEETLE:

Woof Juice! Right again!

STAGE ACTION: FIRE MARSHAL steps briefly onto the stage.

FIRE MARSHAL:

This burn pile is soaking wet. How would you ever get that to burn?

BEETLE:

Oh, you put enough gas on it, anything will burn!

FIRE MARSHAL (hands cupped over ears walking off stage):

I hear nothing. I hear nothing.

SOUND EFFECT: AUDIENCE chuckles.

STAGE ACTION: DANA is appalled at Beetle for saying this.

DANA:

BEETLE! How could you say that to him?! And with such a straight face?

BEETLE (smirking):

Well... he doesn't know I'm not kidding.

BEETLE (to audience):

You see, Woof Juice is a mixture of [BLEEEP] and [BLEEEP].

SOUND EFFECT: Bleeping sound masks over the ingredients as Beetle speaks to them.

BEETLE:

What's that about? What's that BLEEPing sound? I didn't swear or anything. That's censorship!

DANA (chuckling):

Beetle, that isn't censorship, it's COMMON SENSE. Let's just leave some things to the imagination.

BEETLE (to Dana):

Well, OK, if we *have* to.

BEETLE (to audience):

You mix these things up and put it on a brush pile, wet or dry, and it WILL BURN. I call it WOOF JUICE, cuz' it goes WOOF when you light it.

ROGER DUTTWEILER:

Uh uh, NOPE. I'm not in this story.

BEETLE (continuing):

Oh, yes you are! See, you take the Woof Juice and pour it over your wet burn pile and then you just light it and WOOF.

ROGER DUTTWEILER (backing away):

Well, yeah, that is if you don't let it sit there and create a cloud of volatile vapor.

BEETLE (reaching for a lighter):

You ain't going anywhere, Roger! That's where you come in...

STAGE ACTION: An argument breaks out on the stage with Roger and Beetle pointing fingers at each other trying to blame each other for lighting the burn pile.

DANA (to audience):

Right now, as they are fighting about who lit the brush pile, a vapor cloud is building and building. It stores up its energy in the form of unlit gas which will eventually inform an entire town, en masse, of catastrophe.

SOUND EFFECT: BOOM!

STAGE ACTION: An explosion is heard that rattles the theater. ROGER DUTTWEILER claws his way off the stage on his hands and knees.

MEMOIR NARRATION (DANA): Phone calls lit up 911 call centers, town offices, and the local fire departments in choreographed precision that was locked in sync with a concussion wave that traveled out from ground-zero.

STAGE ACTION: Meanwhile BEETLE grabs a rake to lean on it. A FIRE MARSHAL quickly comes onto the scene.

FIRE MARSHAL:

You OK? What was that explosion I just heard?

BEETLE (relaxing on the garden rake):

No, everything is good here. Explosion? I don't know what that was.

FIRE MARSHAL:

Huh, you got a permit for that fire?

BEETLE (reaching into his pocket):

Yup, right here!

FIRE MARSHAL:

Ok, then. Be safe.

MEMOIR NARRATION (DANA): *All over the state of Maine, the ingredients of Woof Juice were banned in a single day. Fire departments would create special Woof Juice Awareness Programs and towns would form special Woof Juice Prevention Councils.*

Most importantly, no one was injured in the infamous Woof Juice incident.

BEETLE (with a long deep sigh):

Aaahhhh.

STAGE ACTION: A stagehand throws something to BEETLE and he catches it in mid air.

BEETLE (coming to himself):

What a sec! Where'd Roger go? I have a t-shirt for him also.

STAGE ACTION: A hand off stage reaches on stage and snatches the shirt.

ROGER (voice offstage chuckling):

SWEET!

STAGE ACTION: ROGER appears with hearing protection and a t-shirt with a graphic of a mushroom cloud that says, 'IT WASN'T ME!' and proudly walks across the stage in front of DANA and BEETLE and steps back into the audience.

SOUND EFFECT: AUDIENCE erupts in laughter again.

BEETLE:

NOW, we can go to ACT V!

End of Scene 21

END OF ACT IV

ACT V
The Final Days.

"Me? Trouble!?"
– Beetle

Scene 22: Heaven and Earth

STAGE ACTION: The stage is split. SPLIT LEFT- Heavenly realm, golden glow, GOD seated in authority, SATAN standing in defiance. SPLIT RIGHT- the hospital room, harsh fluorescent light, BEETLE in bed surrounded by family and friends, machines softly beeping. The tableaus hold still for a breath, then life slowly begins to stir.

SATAN (voice echoing, mocking):

Look at your servant. Strip away his comfort, and he will curse you. He only laughs because you shield him.

GOD (calm, steady, voice resonant):

My servant's joy is not rooted in the comforts of the world, but in Me.

STAGE LIGHTS: Heavenly light deepens, radiating across the divide.

STAGE ACTION: GOD raises His hand, and His words thunder with scripture.

GOD:

"Do not grieve, for the joy of the Lord is your strength."

SOUND EFFECTS: The words echo into the hospital side.

STAGE ACTION: DANA, seated by BEETLE, stirs and glances down at his open journal where the same verse is underlined. His hand rests upon it.

STAGE ACTION: HOSPITAL TABLEAU freezes in a still frame of quiet reverence — BEETLE, weak but faintly smiling, DANA at his side, family holding vigil.

STAGE ACTION: Back in the **HEAVENLY TABLEAU**, SA-TAN recoils slightly at the force of the words, but remains defiant. The golden glow edges into the hospital space, softening the sterile white light.

Both realms hold in tension — Heaven declaring eternal truth, Earth embodying fragile suffering — bound together by the same promise.

STAGE LIGHTS: Lights fade.

Hospital Room

SOUND EFFECTS: Soft beeping of the monitor.

STAGE LIGHTS: Low, steady light over the bed. BEETLE lies propped up against pillows, pale but alert. DANA sits close, adjusting a blanket.

DANA (gentle, steady):

Easy, brother. I've got you.

BEETLE (weak smile):

You always do.

STAGE ACTION: STAGE SPLIT shows MARY ELLEN at her home sitting in her chair.

MARY ELLEN (whispering):

God, give Beetle comfort I pray. Give him strength for each breath.

STAGE ACTION: A pause. DANA reaches to the tray table and picks up a scrambled Rubik's Cube — one of the things he brought along with a Nerf gun and a toy dinosaur to cheer Beetle. He sets it in BEETLE'S hands.

SOUND EFFECT: Click-click. The familiar sound of turns fills the silence.

BEETLE (smirking faintly):

Can't leave it messed up. That'd bug me worse than the cancer.

DANA (grinning through tears):

Figures. Even now, you've got to show me up with your speed at solving the cube.

STAGE ACTION: BEETLE twists deliberately. With shaky precision, he completes the cube, holds it up for a moment, then places it on his lap. Soft laughter ripples through the room, then fades into reverent quiet.

DANA (memoir voice, to audience):

That was Beetle. Even in weakness, joy was his strength. A cube, a joke, a prayer — they became more than distractions. They were his testimony.

STAGE ACTION: DANA gently sets the cube on the bedside table. It remains there, visible, as the lights soften and the tableau freezes.

Cross-Fade Between Realms

STAGE LIGHTS: Heavenly glow on one side, hospital room on the other. Lights overlap, blending realms.

SATAN (mocking):

See how weak he is? He clings to toys like a child.

GOD (firm, resonant):

No. He clings to joy. That is his weapon.

BEETLE (whispering, faint grin):

"The joy of the Lord is my strength."

DANA (tight grip on Beetle's hand, eyes wet):

Amen. From the beginning to the end — take joy in the Lord, brother.

STAGE LIGHTS: Heavenly glow and hospital lights merge into one soft spotlight on BEETLE'S face.

STAGE ACTION: FAMILY TABLEAU frozen in reverence. Heavenly side still in quiet defiance. A breath of silence.

STAGE LIGHTS: Blackout.

Reader's Note: *This moment took place at Eastern Maine Medical Center, June 2023. Visitors brought Beetle playful gifts — a Nerf gun, stuffed dinosaur, and Rubik's Cube — reflecting his humor even in weakness.*

End of Scene 22

Scene 23: My Own Panic Attacks

STAGE LIGHTS: Hospital room, soft and steady. BEETLE lies in bed. VISITORS come and go. Machines hum quietly. DANA sits near him with a journal in hand.

MEMOIR NARRATION (DANA): *Those weeks at the hospital were full of people. Friends, coworkers, even townsfolk came to see Beetle one last time. His body grew weaker, but somehow his humor never did. For me, though, those days brought more than grief — they brought my own battles.*

Vignette 1 – Nerf Gun & Cube

(A *vignette* is a short, self-contained scene that captures a single moment, memory, or impression. In this script, vignettes highlight brief snapshots of Beetle's story without a full scene build.)

STAGE ACTION: BEETLE fumbles under the blanket, pulls out a Nerf gun, and fires weakly at DANA. A toy dinosaur lays on the hospital room floor, having already fallen victim to Nerf bullets. A scrambled Rubik's Cube rests on the tray table.

BEETLE (smiling faintly):

Gotcha.

DANA (dodging, shaking head):

Nope! Still missed. Some things never change.

BEETLE:

No! I definitely got you!

VISITOR (chuckling):

Even flat on your back, you're still trouble.

BEETLE (pointing at DANA):

Me trouble?! It's him! He's trouble!

STAGE ACTION: Light laughter ripples. BEETLE reaches for the Rubik's Cube, turns it a few times with trembling hands, then tosses it back on the tray with a grin.

MEMOIR NARRATION (DANA): That was Beetle — cracking jokes in the face of pain. But when the laughter faded, my own storm returned. Panic pressed hard on my chest. My mind was split: family and work waiting back in North Carolina, and Beetle here, slipping away. I felt like I was failing at both.

Dana's Spiritual Foundation

MEMOIR NARRATION (DANA): Looking back, I see how God had been preparing me. Years earlier, I began handwriting the book of Matthew, then journaling through all 150 Psalms. Page by page, prayer by prayer, He built a reservoir of truth inside me. And now, when anxiety raged, those words became my shield.

STAGE ACTION: DANA opens journal, reads aloud softly.

DANA (reading):

"Father, I cry out like David did. I feel overwhelmed, trapped in deep waters with no escape. Darkness surrounds me. True freedom isn't here, but in You alone. Help me. Remind me — the joy of the Lord is my strength."

Flashback – Workplace Breakdown

STAGE ACTION: Lights shift. DANA stands apart, holding a phone to his ear. Boss's voice offstage.

DANA (strained):

I'm drowning here. Can we pause some projects? Just 30 days. Even without full pay.

BOSS (offstage):

We can't accommodate that.

DANA (erupts):

Then I QUIT!

STAGE ACTION: DANA slams the phone down, breath ragged. Lights fade back to the hospital room.

Return to Hospital

MEMOIR NARRATION (DANA): Even quitting didn't bring relief. Anxiety stalked me everywhere. I kept writing, kept praying, because I didn't know what else to do. And yet, God used those words to anchor me. He reminded me I wasn't carrying Beetle alone. He was carrying us both. Though I tried to quit, my boss wouldn't let me. I'm sure they sensed some sort of war going on inside me, so I continued struggling in my personal life and work, day after day.

DANA:

Hey Beetle, it was a long trip, I think I'm gonna take a nap.

BEETLE:

Yeah, go ahead. I don't plan on going anywhere.

STAGE ACTION: DANA drifts off into sleep.

End of Scene 23

Scene 24: The Trip to Beetle

STAGE LIGHTS: DANA at a desk in North Carolina. Papers scattered. Suitcase open. Phone in hand. Lighting shifts between office, car headlights, and hotel room as the journey unfolds.

Opening – Memoir Frame

MEMOIR NARRATION (DANA): On June 13th, I tried to go back to work, but my heart pounded louder with every mile to the office. I didn't want to be there. I needed to be in Maine with my best friend. Beetle was now at Eastern Maine Medical Center in Bangor — too sick for the smaller hospital to handle. Deep down, I knew the time was short.

I lingered in North Carolina for days, torn between duty and the pull of family. But my chest never calmed. Every sunrise made the choice clearer: I couldn't stay away.

Phone Call – Wednesday, June 14th

STAGE ACTION: DANA paces with phone.

DANA (into phone):

Hey man, any updates?

BEETLE (weak, offstage voice):

They've taken blood. They still don't know what's going on.

DANA (swallows hard):

Then I'm on my way.

MEMOIR NARRATION (DANA): Everything became clear at that moment. Work could wait. Beetle could not. My workplace understood — for that, I was grateful. I packed a bag, kissed Angela and the boys, and hit the road.

Flashback – Previous Hospitalization

MEMOIR NARRATION (DANA): It wasn't the first time. Just months earlier, Beetle nearly died from infection. But this was different. Somehow it was even more serious. As I drove north, an unease gnawed at me. My chest tightened, and I knew: this might be one of our final journeys together.

Road Sequence – Prayers & Journaling

STAGE ACTION: Projection of headlights moving across stage. DANA grips the wheel, then kneels at a hotel bed with the Bible and journal open.

MEMOIR NARRATION (DANA): Eight hours on the road gave me too much time to think. By nightfall in Pennsylvania, I stopped, prayed, and wrote in my journal. Panic stalked me even there, but writing gave me breath between suffocating emotions.

DANA (reading journal softly):

"Father, You know every part of us. Please give Beetle strength today. Baffle the doctors with his progress. Calm my chest, calm my mind. All blessings belong to You. *The joy of the Lord is my strength.*"

Arrival at Hospital

STAGE LIGHTS: Whiteboard projection: *Name: Stephen. Goes By: Beetle.* DANA enters Beetle's hospital room. BEETLE sits slumped in a chair, head low. A Rubik's Cube rests unsolved on the tray table.

DANA:

Beetle!

STAGE ACTION: DANA rushes forward, hugs him gently.

BEETLE (faint smile):

How was the trip?

DANA (steadying voice):

Uneventful. But I needed to be here.

MEMOIR NARRATION (DANA): *That was Beetle. Always asking about others first, even while he suffered. Classic Beetle.*

Doctor & Nurse Interaction

STAGE ACTION: NURSE adjusts IV. The DOCTOR enters with a chart.

NURSE:

Beetle, let's try a little water.

BEETLE (weak grin):

I'll try.

DOCTOR (to Dana):

Are you family?

BEETLE (firm, despite weakness):

He's my best friend. Give him updates.

MEMOIR NARRATION (DANA): *Those words carried more weight than I could hold. Best friend. It was permission, trust, and love wrapped in one sentence.*

Closing Reflection

MEMOIR NARRATION (DANA): *From that moment on, I was fixed at his side. North Carolina was far away; this was where I was called to be. God had prepared me — through Scripture, through prayer, even through panic. And now, every mile, every page, every tear had brought me here… to walk my brother through his final stretch.*

STAGE LIGHTS: Lights dim on Beetle and Dana. A soft glow rests on the Rubik's Cube at his bedside.

STAGE ACTION: DANA wakes from his flashback to find himself in the reality of a hospital room. None of it was a dream—it was all REAL.

Reader's Note: *This moment took place in June 2023. Dana drove from North Carolina to Bangor, Maine, to be with Beetle during his final hospitalization at Eastern Maine Medical Center.*

End of Scene 24

Scene 25: Rubik's Cube

STAGE LIGHTS: A gentle spotlight falls across the hospital bed. The hum of machines underscores the silence.

STAGE ACTION (SILENT TABLEAU):

(A *silent tableau* is a staged "living picture" where actors freeze in place without speaking. The silence focuses the audience on posture, expression, and the visual storytelling of the moment.)

1. BEETLE lies propped up, pale but alert.

2. He reaches for the Rubik's Cube on the bedside table — the same one seen in earlier days.

3. His hands tremble, but he works the cube with deliberate focus.

4. DANA sits nearby, journal open, his pen hovering mid-sentence as he notices.

5. A FEW VISITORS gather at the edge of the room, whispering, then falling silent as they watch.

6. Click by click, the colors align.

7. At last, with a soft snap, the cube is complete.

8. BEETLE exhales, a faint smile breaking across his face. He raises the solved cube with quiet triumph.

9. DANA leans forward, eyes wet, one hand pressed to his heart in silent admiration.

Reflective Narration

MEMOIR NARRATION (DANA): *That little cube was Beetle's trademark — puzzles, formulas, challenges he refused to leave unsolved. Even here, when his body shook and his strength failed, he would not surrender the fight.*

Turn by turn, color after color, I realized it wasn't just about the cube. It was about his life. Determined. Patient. Unwilling to quit.

And in that moment, as he held the solved puzzle with a faint smile, I saw Scripture come alive: "I have fought the good fight, I have finished the race, I have kept the faith." (2 Timothy 4:7)

Broken body, steady spirit. Always finishing what he started. Always finishing in Christ.

TABLEAU FREEZES:

Beetle holding the solved cube aloft; Dana watching with a hand over his heart; visitors standing reverent and still.

STAGE LIGHTS: Dim to Blackout.

Reader's Note: *This moment took place at Eastern Maine Medical Center, June 2023. Even in his final days, Beetle's humor and determination endured; the solved Rubik's Cube became a symbol of perseverance, joy, and faith in suffering.*

End of Scene 25

Scene 26: Tall Tales

STAGE LIGHTS: Same hospital room. The solved Rubik's Cube rests on the bedside table, catching the soft light.

Beetle's Story

BEETLE (weak but animated, to visitors):

Did I ever tell you about the time that Dana and I convinced a kid at camp that we'd captured bigfoot and shoved him in the boathouse?

VISITOR (rolling eyes, laughing):

Sounds like you guys!

BEETLE (laughing):

Turns out the kid's dad was there at camp as well and the kid runs off saying, 'Wait until I tell my dad you got bigfoot, he isn't going to believe it!'

STAGE ACTION: Visitors chuckle, shaking their heads.

DANA (aside, memoir voice):

Every story he told I had heard a thousand times. But lying there, frail and fighting, somehow the stories felt more real.

DANA (whispering to himself):

Will this be the last time I get to hear Beetle tell that story? How many stories are left in his well of humor?

Reaction

VISITOR (to Dana, shaking head):

Still spinning yarns, huh?

DANA (smiling, softly):

Yes, proficiently! And somehow, they keep getting better.

Memoir Reflection

DANA (stepping forward, memoir narration, solemn):

That was Beetle. Even as his body weakened, his stories grew larger than life. He gave us laughter in greater proportion than our tears. Humor was his gift — one last way of carrying us, when we thought we were there to carry him.

STAGE ACTION: DANA glances toward the Rubik's Cube on the table.

And maybe that was the point. Humor and perseverance, side by side. His weapon wasn't just strength, nor did he live in denial — it was joy.

STAGE LIGHTS: Lights dim.

Reader's Note: *This moment took place at Eastern Maine Medical Center, June 2023. Beetle continued sharing his trademark tall tales, bringing laughter to friends and family in the midst of loss.*

End of Scene 26

Scene 27- Grace for the Last Mile

STAGE ACTION: ANGELA walks on stage into the hospital room with her cell phone in hand laughing.

VISITOR:

What are you watching?

ANGELA (chuckling):

You gotta see this video of Beetle and Dana Bigfoot Hunting!

STAGE ACTION: VISITORS crowd around ANGELA with her phone as she plays a clip of the Squatchin' video of Dana and Beetle.

PHONE AUDIO (Beetle's voice):

"If you are one with nature, nature will be one with you… and I've lived my life by that principle ever since."

DANA (to audience):

And you can watch that video to this day by going to tinyurl.com/ bigfoothunt—that is if you want a good laugh!

STAGE ACTION: The room of visitors erupts with laughter. BEE-TLE smirks looking over to DANA.

SOUND EFFECT: Knock, knock.

STAGE ACTION: NURSE and DOCTOR enter.

NURSE (asking DANA):

Can we clear out the room for a few minutes? I need to take Beetle's vitals and the doctor is here as well.

STAGE ACTION: Everyone but DANA and ANGELA, leave the room to give the NURSE and DOCTOR some space.

DOCTOR:

Uh, Beetle. I'm told that's what you go by. How are you feeling today?

BEETLE (as nurse takes BEETLE's blood pressure):

Well, I've been better.

STAGE ACTION: ANGELA and DANA gather with their best friend putting their arms around his back and face the doctor, joining forces to sustain the blow they all know is coming.

DOCTOR:

That's understandable. It seems that we finally know what is going on and it isn't good. What we know now from your labs and tests is that you have stage four stomach and throat cancer.

BEETLE (swallowing hard):

So what does that mean?

DOCTOR (delivering words gently):

I'm going to be completely honest. It means that we finally understand why your organs are shutting down and it means that you don't have months, or even weeks to live. You only have a few days. Do you understand what I am saying?

STAGE ACTION: BEETLE nods his head.

DANA (pulling closer to Beetle):

Remember when I ran 50 miles on my 50th birthday? Well, that was tough, but I want you to know that whatever this race holds, we are going to finish it together.

MEMOIR NARRATION (DANA): *And the race ahead would be challenging. But God gave grace, mercy, and love for every step of the battle to come.*

ANGELA (through tears):

Beetle, you're gonna beat us all to be with Jesus.

STAGE ACTION: BEETLE nods at ANGELA with a solemn look.

DOCTOR (continuing):

But the good news is that we are finally going to get you home.

STAGE ACTION: BEETLE smiles uncontrollably and starts to get up as if the doctor's words are permission to leave.

NURSE:

Not so fast, Beetle, we still need to get you all unhooked.

BEETLE (voice in a whisper):

Finally, I can get home to Max and Bigfoot!

DOCTOR:

Who are they?

DANA (answering for his best friend):

They are his pets.

DOCTOR:

Well, that will be good then. Sounds like we need to get you home as soon as possible. I'm going to turn things over to this nurse who will brief you on everything that will be happening and get you unhooked as we make every effort to get you home as soon as possible.

STAGE ACTION: DOCTOR walks out.

NURSE:

Ok, Beetle, here's what we are going to do…

STAGE ACTION: NURSE continues and DANA steps in front of their ongoing conversation.

DANA (with a big sigh to the audience):

Being completely honest with you, what you just saw was my hardest moment of my life to this day. Running 50 miles on my 50th birthday didn't hold a candle to this moment in time. That day, running those 50 miles, I clearly remember mile 43, when I was at rock bottom. My energy was sucked dry and I still had miles to go. My legs felt like cement, yet I had to continue to push. In similarity, the words we just received hung in the air and their weight was like cement. But I now had a very clear mission. I had to help make sure we got Beetle home and help him cross the finish line.

End of Scene 27

END OF ACT V

ACT VI
The Homecoming.

"Just making sure
you are still there."
– Beetle

Scene 28: The Big One-Liner

STAGE LIGHTS: Hospital room. DANA sits at Beetle's bedside with one or two visitors gathered. A mood of half-laughter, half-silence lingers.

MEMOIR NARRATION (DANA): *While Beetle waits to be unhooked from all the hospital gadgets, light-heartedness continues in the midst of a desperate situation, a situation that will deliver the ultimate Beetle one-liner.*

Build-Up

VISITOR (chuckling, finishing a funny story):

...and that's when the canoe tipped, and we all went swimming in April!

DANA (laughing, wiping eyes):

Oh man, I'd forgotten about that one. We froze for days.

SOUND EFFECT: Monitor beeps steadily. The room holds a fragile mix of laughter and exhaustion.

MEMOIR NARRATION (DANA): *Visitors begin getting a little louder with laughter while telling each other Beetle stories. But then there was a line from Beetle that cut through the waves of laughter like lightning.*

The room bursts with laughter as someone just finished a classic story.

Beetle's Climax Line

BEETLE (suddenly blurts, raspy voice, but with that mischievous grin):

I'm dyin' over here... and you guys are tellin' jokes!

SOUND EFFECT: Beat of stunned silence. Then the room bursts into laughter — bittersweet, too loud for a hospital room.

STAGE ACTION: DANA leans forward, gripping BEETLE'S hand tightly, caught between tears and laughter. `

MEMOIR NARRATION (DANA): That was it, it was a classic Beetle mic drop moment. We all, Beetle included, exploded in laughter far too loudly for hospital room etiquette. The laughter then dissolved into tears and long sighs of relief. In one line, Beetle gave us permission to hold both — the comedy and the tragedy — side by side. It became a line, cemented into us just as the name Beetle had become cemented into Stephen.

Memoir Reflection

DANA (stepping forward, memoir voice, softer, past tense):

It was the line of a lifetime. Humor, honesty, and heartbreak in one breath. He broke the tension in that room, gave us permission to laugh even as death stood at the door.

That was Beetle — refusing to let suffering have the last word. His strength was joy, the very joy Scripture speaks of: *"The joy of the Lord is your strength."* (Nehemiah 8:10) Even here, even then, joy was his defiance.

And I heard another echo in that moment, words I'd known since childhood: *"I have fought the good fight, I have finished the race, I have kept the faith."* (2 Timothy 4:7)

He was telling us: death doesn't win.

STAGE LIGHTS: Spotlight narrows to BEETLE'S smile, then fades into the quiet hum of monitors.

STAGE LIGHTS: Blackout.

Reader's Note: *This moment took place at Eastern Maine Medical Center, June 2023. Beetle's words, "I'm dyin' over here and you guys are tellin' jokes," became a lasting memory of his humor in the face of death.*

End of Scene 28

Scene 29 - Home

MEMOIR NARRATION (DANA): Getting Beetle home was no small feat. Due to help from Marilyn Stoddard and others, Beetle's house was properly prepared for him to come home—a bedroom being specifically prepared for him on the main floor of his simple two-story home. Yet, finally, through the diligence of so many, Beetle was finally delivered back to his home at 152 Maple Street in Danforth, Maine.

STAGE ACTION: TWO MEN from an ambulance help move BEETLE into a bed.

BEETLE (with a big smile):

Ahhh. So good to be home! Get over here, Max!

STAGE ACTION: Max comes over, tail wagging.

STAGE ACTION: DANA, ANGELA, and others gather around BEETLE making sure he is comfortable.

ANGELA:

How are you doing, Beetle? Any pain or anything?

BEETLE:

Nope, I just feel uncomfortable in my stomach, but no pain.

MEMOIR NARRATION (DANA): And that is how it was right to the end. No pain, just some discomfort causing him to lean forward.

End of Scene 29

Scene 30: Reminiscing

STAGE LIGHTS: BEETLE now home. There is a soft glow. Beetle reclines weakly in bed. DANA sits beside him with a journal. A few visitors lean close, listening.

MEMOIR NARRATION (DANA): *Beetle's voice was weak, but his memory stayed sharp. We slipped back into our rhythm — I'd forget details, and he'd correct me. We laughed through story after story and everyone was much more relaxed knowing Beetle was home.*

End of Scene 30

Scene 31: Visitors

MEMOIR NARRATION (DANA): *Then the flood gates opened. Yes, there were many visitors at the hospital, but what happened in the next couple days eclipsed the visitors at the hospital.*

VISITOR 1:

Hey Beetle! What are you doing here in bed?

BEETLE:

Oh, I dunno, just hanging around I guess.

VISITOR 2:

Hey Beetle! You comin' to work today or what?

BEETLE:

No, I think I'll be out for a while.

VISITOR 3:

Hey Beetle! Remember that time…

MEMOIR NARRATION (DANA): *That's right, Beetle got home on a Monday and Tuesday, Wednesday, and Thursday were flooded with visitors. They just kept streaming in. About 50 of them over three days. With each visitor, Beetle's realization of his impact on this little community grew stronger and stronger. Memories reinforced. Stories retold. Faith strengthened. Angela and my days were filled with, "Beetle, Mary Ellen is here to visit" and "Beetle, Pastor Pete is here to visit."*

ANGELA

Beetle, Dave Conley is here to visit.

BEETLE (smiles and in a shallow whisper):

Hey, Dave.

DAVE:

Man, Beetle, you remember all those pranks you played on me?

BEETLE (unrelenting):

Who? Me?

DAVE:

Yeah, right, 'who me?!'

BEETLE (smirking):

Just remember, you are the one that dented my trombone.

DAVE (chuckling):

Who me?

BEETLE:

Yeah, right, 'WHO ME?!'

MEMOIR NARRATION (DANA): Each visitor, one by one, tied off their relationship with Beetle in some way. Maybe they did so with eyes wide open, or unknowingly, but each left something in Beetle's house, a part of them that would never be retrieved again. But they also took something that day.

STAGE ACTION: Beetle's brothers, JIMMY and MARK, walk onto the stage and into the scene and sit with BEETLE.

JIMMY:

Aren't you mad about all this?

BEETLE (in clarity):

Nope.

STAGE ACTION: MARK sits and chats with BEETLE telling stories of childhood and JIMMY takes ANGELA and DANA aside in the hallway.

JIMMY (to Dana):

Unbelievable. If I was in his shoes, I'd be bitter, angry, furious. Losing Dad, losing Chris, losing Mum. But Beetle? Having to go through all this he doesn't seem the slightest bit mad at God. Amazing.

DANA:

Jimmy, I can tell you honestly, in all this, Beetle hasn't once shaken his fist at God in anger. What you see here, the humor, the smiles, the joy, he's had this from day one in the hospital. I agree. Amazing. But it shows where his faith lies, doesn't it?

JIMMY:

It sure does. When I go, I want to go like that!

MEMOIR NARRATION (DANA): *THAT was what everyone took away. Even though everyone left part of themselves knowing that they would unlikely see Beetle again on this earth, they took away hope. Yes, everyone took away hope. Angela and I conversed with Jimmy and Mark, astounded by Beetle's perseverance, who also wanted to ensure that Angela and I were okay. I continued to praise God for that hidden strength, unrelenting, to which Beetle held fast and held fast in me as well. The flurry of visitors subsided. Beetle's condition worsened, which was totally expected according to the nurse's instructions for the final days.*

Hey, Mark!

MEMOIR NARRATION (DANA): *Over the remaining days, we would have occasional visitors, but would spend time outside as well, pushing Beetle in a wheelchair to get fresh air. Night was the hardest push, but Angela had that covered.*

ANGELA:

What do you want to listen to tonight?

BEETLE (in a raspy whisper):

Third Day.

ANGELA:

You got it.

MEMOIR NARRATION (DANA): White Heart. The Kry. Petra. Whatever Beetle wanted, she'd put on the radio. Then, Angela would sit there, leaning on Beetle's bed, taking short naps in between helping Beetle shift from one side of the bed to the other to help him keep as comfortable as possible.

STAGE ACTION: BEETLE, facing away from Angela, reaches behind his back

ANGELA (reaching to touch his hand):

What do you need, Beetle?

BEETLE:

Oh, nothing, just making sure you are still there.

Long pause.

MEMOIR NARRATION (DANA): Then it happened again.

BEETLE:

I need to get up and sit in the chair.

ANGELA:

Well, Mark Barlett is here tonight with me, let me see if he will help.

BEETLE:

OK.

ANGELA (calling to Mark in a half-whisper):

Hey, Mark.

BEETLE:

That'll never work. You gotta do it like this…

MEMOIR NARRATION (DANA): I hit pause for a second so you re-alize the gravity of what happened next. At this point, Beetle's voice was barely a whisper. He had kept clearing his dry throat to say anything, but just like that, clear as a bell and at full volume…

BEETLE (with a loud yell):

HEY, MARK, GET IN HERE!

STAGE ACTION: MARK appears at Beetle's door as if snapped over like a bungy cord.

MEMOIR NARRATION (DANA): It seemed that one by one, all of the important things of life tied themselves off in those final days. Such was this case.

SOUND EFFECTS: Knock, knock.

STAGE ACTION: ANGELA opens the door.

ANGELA (sharing a hug and a tear with the visitor):

Thank you for coming!

MEMOIR NARRATION (DANA): All the helpers then hear the warm-est greeting of all time.

AMANDA:

BEETLE! How are you!?

BEETLE (with a smile unshaken by cancer):

Oh, pretty good! How are you?

MEMOIR NARRATION (DANA): It was an unmistakable moment of time for all that got to witness it. A blast from the past, from years at Living Waters, colliding together with the present.

THE BIG SHOW

MEMOIR NARRATION (DANA): It was July 1st at 6:00 AM. I arrived back at Beetle's to help give Angela and Mark Barlett a break. Janet, Angela's mother, was there. Mark was headed home to get some rest. Amanda also was getting rest.

DANA:

How is he doing?

ANGELA:

I didn't get much sleep at all. He tossed and turned all night.

DANA:

Well, get rest, I'll stay here.

STAGE ACTION: JANET stays in the room with BEETLE as ANGELA and DANA chat.

ANGELA:

It's interesting, so often he points to the corner of the room as if he sees something. He'll be laying there, then suddenly reach out his hand. He looks so intently, I wonder if somehow, he sees the other side.

DANA:

I don't know, but he can't continue to hang on much longer like this.

JANET:

Dana, Angela, you should probably come in.

MEMOIR NARRATION (DANA): *Janet was quite familiar with the final moments of life, having worked in hospice care for many years.*

JANET:

He's taking long breaths, I think this is it.

STAGE ACTION: DANA and ANGELA take Beetle's hand, JANET places her hand on his shoulder.

STAGE ACTION: BEETLE exhaled long.

JANET:

He's gone.

MEMOIR NARRATION (DANA): *The time was 6:14 AM on July 1ˢᵗ, 2023. When his final breath came, the room changed. It was as though heaven leaned in close, and time itself stopped. Silence fell, heavy yet holy. Beetle was gone, but the peace that filled the room was undeniable. In a moment that felt heavy and long, heaven and earth made an exchange. A soul departed from one and entered the other. From death to life. From the temporal world to the eternal.*

DANA (through tears):

We need to give this moment to the Lord.

STAGE ACTION: JANET and ANGELA sob quietly.

DANA:

Father, we thank you for the moments we had with Beetle. We thank you for his love, his laughter, his friendship. We don't know why he had to go, but we thank you that he was not bitter once during this experience. Please extend your peace to his family and friends and may all see Beetle's life as a testimony for you as we have. We praise you.

MEMOIR NARRATION (DANA): *Silence fell, heavy yet holy. Beetle was gone, but the peace that filled the room was undeniable. Peace. Peace. Peace.*

STAGE ACTION: DANA rises slowly, takes the solved Rubik's Cube from the bedside table, and lays it gently on Beetle's chest, but keeps his hand on the cube.

STAGE LIGHTS: A soft spotlight lingers on BEETLE'S face, calm in stillness.

DANA (TO AUDIENCE):

I had walked with him through laughter, mischief, trials, and countless memories. And now I walked with him to the edge of eternity where I had to let go, but he was permitted to continue. Beetle had reflected God's humor, God's joy, and finally, God's peace.

That birthday, running those 50 miles, I dare not leave out a substantial fact: It was mile 43, I was exhausted, dehydrated, it was 93 degrees. It seemed hopeless. The sky was ominous and threatening. Then, in a moment, it opened up in rain that cooled my overheated body. It was a rain that refreshed my spirit and I finished that 50-miler strong.

Now, with Beetle, once again, rain opened up. This time in the form of tears and overwhelming peace.

STAGE ACTION: DANA picks the cube once again and walks to the empty stool which was never moved from the stage and places it on the empty stool. The light dim, except for a small circle of light on the Rubik's cube, a shadow of what remained of Beetle. He solved it.

DANA (TO AUDIENCE):

And I remembered the words of Scripture: *"I have fought the good fight, I have finished the race, I have kept the faith."* (2 Timothy 4:7)

That was Beetle's life — and that was his finish.

STAGE LIGHTS: Lights dim to blackout.

Reader's Note: *Stephen "Beetle" Bailey passed away at home in Danforth, Maine on July 1ˢᵗ, 2025 at 6:14 A.M. He was surrounded by Dana and Angela Morrison and Janet Perkins (Angela's mother).*

End of Scene 31

END OF ACT VI

Epilogue
THE CURTAIN FALLS, THE LEGACY LIVES ON

STAGE LIGHTS: Bare stage. A single spotlight on DANA at center stage. The Rubik's Cube remains on the stool, bathed in soft light.

MEMOIR NARRATION (DANA): *The strength that Beetle carried cries out to you. Will you hear it? The destiny of the frail body we all have is the same. We all die, yet why do we hold such fear for death?*

"For all have sinned and fall short of the glory of God." (Romans 3:23)

Beetle knew that truth. But he also knew the greater truth — "For the wages of sin is death, but the gift of God is eternal life in Christ Jesus our Lord." (Romans 6:23)

That was the foundation of his joy. His life was not perfect, but it was faithful. He ran his race, and he finished with joy.

DANA (turning to audience, present tense):

We called him Beetle. He showed us that humor heals, kindness matters, and faith endures. Love never ends, and joy outlasts sorrow.

STAGE ACTION: *Pauses, voice softens.*

And if you hear laughter in the quiet places… maybe it's all of us, carrying the same joy as Beetle carried. We too, trudge through the mire of life and have the same opportunity to yield it to Christ.

STAGE ACTION: Dana slowly exits. Spotlight remains on the Rubik's Cube.

A faint echo of 2 Timothy 4:7 is heard as voiceover:

"I have fought the good fight. I have finished the race. I have kept the faith."

STAGE LIGHTS: Blackout.

Reader's Note: *Epilogue: The Curtain Falls, The Legacy Lives On. Beetle's story does not end in July 2023. His laughter, service, and faith live on in the lives of those he touched. His legacy remains, echoing in every memory retold, every act of kindness, and every word of Scripture shared. His joy pointed not to himself but to Christ — and his race finished in faith.*

The Invitation of Joy

Beetle's life was marked by laughter, kindness, and faith — but most of all by the joy he found in Christ. That same joy is offered to you. Scripture says:

> *"For all have sinned and fall short of the glory of God."* (Romans 3:23)

> *"The wages of sin is death, but the gift of God is eternal life in Christ Jesus our Lord."* (Romans 6:23)

> *"If you declare with your mouth, 'Jesus is Lord,' and believe in your heart that God raised him from the dead, you will be saved."* (Romans 10:9)

Beetle believed these truths — and they gave him peace even in his final breath. You can share in that same peace today. Beetle's story was one of laughter, but his testimony was of salvation. That same gift — that same joy — is offered to you.

Do you recognize that you have fallen short of God's glory?

Do you realize Jesus came, died, and rose again on behalf of your wrongdoing?

Do you receive that gift of life he extends so graciously to you?

There are no magic words, just talk to him and receive his gift of life!

Seeking Jesus Christ

Do you desire Christ and long to be part of God's family? If you asked Jesus to be your Lord and Savior, here are some next steps to help you grow in your new faith:

- **Tell Someone** – Share your decision with a trusted Christian friend, pastor, or family member. Joy grows when it's shared.

- **Read God's Word** – Start with the Gospel of John in the New Testament. Let God's promises encourage and guide you each day.

- **Pray Daily** – Talk to God honestly, as you would a close friend. Thank Him, ask for help, and listen in the quiet.

- **Be Obedient to Scripture** – As you learn from God's Word what He desires of you, practice it, in full obedience to him.

- **Find a Church Family** – Attend a Bible-believing church where you can worship, learn, and walk alongside others in faith.

- **Keep Growing in Joy** – Faith is a journey. Like Beetle, let Scripture, laughter, and love shape your life as a testimony of God's grace.

Lastly, if your faith has been strengthened by Beetle's story, then I would love to hear from you. I hope you will take the time to reach out by emailing dana@beetlebook.com and let me know how this book has impacted your life. Of course, if you knew Beetle, you could throw in a story or two as well!

Last Words

Now, let me share with you some words from some people that knew Beetle well.

Mark Bailey: "I think it's important to emphasize where Beetle got his humor. Every Sunday, our dad [Jimmy Sr.] would say, 'Let's go! It's time to go to church.' Beetle would say, 'I can't find my shoes!' or 'I can't find my socks!' or 'I can't find my belt!' Our dad would say, 'Well, just put them on and we'll look for them later! We gotta go to church!'" Beetle would yell, "How can I put them on if I don't know where they are?!" continuing, Mark adds, "But Beetle had a giving heart like my mom. She would give to anyone in need making clothes for them or giving various things to them, he was like that as well."

Jimmy Bailey: "When Steve was fifteen, he and dad [Jimmy Sr.] had an altercation. Steve stormed off to his room with dad close behind. Dad poked and prodded Steve telling him who the boss was and how life worked. Steve replied, 'Get out of my room!' Dad said, 'It's my house!' Steve replied with, 'I'm leaving!' Dad came back with 'You will have to go through me!' Dad stood right in the doorway and wasn't a small man. Stephen then grabbed dad gently, yet firmly, and picked him up about a foot off the ground and moved him out of the doorway and left. Dad said to us, 'What will I do? We told him what he WASN'T going to do!'" In a serious tone, Jimmy then says, 'When it came to Stephen's death, he was strong to the end and wasn't bitter. He lived the life [of faith]. Dad lived it, Stephen lived it. I hope that when it comes to my turn, I can handle the challenge like Stephen."

Fred and Kristi Parker: Kristi recalls, "Beetle was an amazing cook. Even while not making big batches of chicken noodle soup for Living Waters, he'd make us some. It was good stuff!"

Lorraine Springer: "Beetle was a good guy... A REALLY good guy. He loved animals and was loved by Lady Bird, Mary Ellen's African Greg parrot.

Jesse Gray: "Working with Beetle for 7 summers at Living Waters brought so many great memories. He had a gift for turning the mundane into something hilarious—like the day we were herding the pigs to their new pen. It was chaotic, but Beetle's laughter made it fun. It didn't hurt that a staff member rode a pig that day! I miss him a lot but I thank God for the joy and friendship he brought into my life."

Marilyn Stoddard: "My friend, Beetle, had a servant's heart. He was quick witted and could make you laugh even when you didn't want to. He was always willing to help no matter what was going on. His compassion for others shone throughout his life. A humble man with such strength—it was his unspoken strength that spoke volumes. His presence alone could bring joy and definitely laughter. I never heard him complain, not even once- well maybe that one time when I threw out his onion plant that was dead. He was a light taken too soon but never forgotten. It was never goodbye but always "see yah later". Someday it will be later and what a reunion we're going to have."

David Faulkner and Juli Grass: "When we purchased Dave's Hardware, Beetle was a permanent fixture and a tremendous help. He knew the vendors and worked with us to organize and upgrade the store. He was a great asset and friend. He was knowledgeable, well liked, always available, dependable and full of great stories. Whenever he was asked the total due for a purchase his answer was always 'A Thoooousand dollars.' Beetle has touched the hearts of many and is sorely missed."

James Carson: "Beetle was my first staff boss at Living Waters, then a co-laborer, a roommate for two summers, and over time, a trusted friend. We would build the Thursday night campfires together, then head off to Karen's for a Jones soda while chapel wrapped up—talking, laughing, and soaking in the quiet. He was a strong Christian—steady and faithful—with a sharp mind for movie lines and a work ethic that never quit. He loved the camp he called home and served with his whole heart. Even after years apart, reconnecting was always easy—just like picking up where we left off."

Carrie Oliver: "Beetle was driving a bus for us [the school in Danforth] and we had a major snow storm. Beetle hadn't come back from his run, so we called and called on the radio and heard nothing. Finally, a student called and said, 'We are on Reservation Road in a ditch.' I asked, 'Where's Beetle?' The student said, 'He's out trying to get the bus unstuck.' So, I get out there and there's Beetle with a shovel and I asked, 'What happened?' He said, 'Well... I left the road.'" She says with a laugh and continues, "Then I asked, 'You good?' He said, 'Yeah, it's gonna take a while to get out.' When I offered to get a tow truck he said, 'No, I got it.' We did end up getting a tow truck to get the bus out. When I asked him about it at the office he said, 'Well, I knew that tow truck was going to be awfully expensive, and I didn't want anyone to be mad, so I thought I'd shovel it out.' That's the kind of determination Beetle had."

John and Dolly Bridgan: Dolly recounts, "It was 1999 and a Sunday morning. We were in church. I told Beetle's mother, Lynn, who was visiting, that I'd like to meet that guy John. John had been helping at Living Waters. Lynn said, 'Oh, Beetle will introduce you!' Lynn told Beetle and he introduced me to John, and we got married later that year! Beetle knew everyone and was a super nice guy. We all miss him."

Stephanie Franklin: "If you ever fell off a forklift, would you keep your cool? I sure wouldn't! But Beetle did one day at work." Stephanie says with laughter in her voice. "So funny! Man, it was hysterical to watch him lose his footing and flop off that machine! Who laughs at things like that?! And he never let me live that down. I was laughing at a man who almost broke his legs." She says in an embarrassed giggle. Continuing, "Beetle used a pair of vice grips as a door handle for his truck when the original handle broke… creative guy. But something I will never forget is that he made a point to come to my house to give me a dollar he owed me. You heard that right, a *dollar*. Beetle was just nice to have around. He was always full of joy and looking to make people smile."

Dave Conley: "I was Bettle's youth pastor back in the 80s when Beetle was a teenager. When we prayed in small groups, I remember Beetle's prayers were simple, relational and sincere in nature. It reminds me of the pharisee and tax payer's prayers in Luke 18."

Mary Ellen Whiteman: "Someone asked Beetle, 'How come you guys don't have any cops in Danforth?' He lifted up his shirt and revealed a sidearm and asked, 'Who needs cops?'" (Note: he was legally carrying a firearm.) Mary Ellen continues, "Beetle was a warm and friendly man who was exceptionally kind to Stan and myself. He loved Lady Bird, our African Gray parrot, and he was always available to help anytime we had issues."

Gerald and Pamela Morrison: Beetle could figure a way to get things done in unique ways. He had his own brand of humor that kept you laughing while waiting for the punch line. He made a hutch to thank me for helping him in English. It means a lot to me - I still use it today. Beetle loved his Savior Jesus Christ and showed it by always willing to give of his time to help others. After working at Living Waters Camp for a summer he said, "This is where I am going to be after High School." He was right.

Pray Like It Matters

Dive Deep in God's Word

www.rocksolidjournals.com

Your Journey to a Rock Solid Faith.

Beetle had a profound impact on those he worked with at **Down On The Farm Maine Wreaths**. He is missed tremendously by all.

- **Handcrafted in Maine**
- **Full & Fragrant**
- **Perfect for Gifting**
- **Made Fresh & Shipped Daily**
- **Shipped Across USA!**
- **Custom Orders Welcome!**

wreathsfrommaine.com
1-888-448-7752